A Guide to
Zebra Finches
THEIR COLOUR VARIETIES, MANAGEMENT & BREEDING

By Milton, John and Joan Lewis

© **2000 ABK Publications**

All rights reserved. No part of this publication may be reproduced, stored in any retrieval system, or transmitted in any form or by any means without the prior permission in writing of the publisher.

**First Published 2000 by
ABK Publications
PO Box 6288,
South Tweed Heads,
NSW. 2486. Australia.**

ISBN 0 9577024 2 6

Front Cover:
Top left: Marked White Zebra Finch cock.
Centre left: Fawn Zebra Finch cock.
Centre right: Cream-backed Zebra Finch cock.
Bottom left: Normal Pied Zebra Finch cock.
Bottom right: Normal Grey Zebra Finch cock.
Back Cover: Australian Isabel Zebra Finch cock.

All photographs by or supplied by Milton & John Lewis except where shown.
All paintings by Joan Lewis.

Design, Type and Art: PrintHouse Multimedia Graphics (Gold Coast)
Colour Separations: Nu Scan (Gold Coast)
Printing: Prestige Litho (Brisbane)

CONTENTS

ABOUT THE AUTHORS	Page 5
ACKNOWLEDGEMENTS	6
INTRODUCTION	8
HISTORY AND ECOLOGY	8
Description of the Wild Zebra Finch	9
How Zebra Finches Live in the Wild	10
HOUSING	**11**
Cabinets	11
Aviaries	12
Construction Materials	14
Aviary Floors	15
Perches	15
Water Vessels	15
Nestboxes	16
Pests	16
Breeding	17
Ringing (Banding)	18
Security	18
FEEDING	**19**
Breeding Season	19
Non-Breeding Season	21
Food Storage	21
HEALTH OF THE ZEBRA FINCH	**22**
A Few Simple Rules	22
Good Husbandry Techniques	23
How Do You Know if Your Birds are Unwell?	24
Zoonosis	24
Psittacosis	
What to Do if a Bird Dies	25
Worming Program	25
Care of Sick Birds	26
Respiratory Disease	26
Diarrhoea	27
Coccidiosis	27
Scaly-face (Scaly-leg)	28
Lice and Mites	28
Feather Plucking	28
Toxins and Poisons	28
Eye Injury and Infections	29
Fractures	29
Do My Birds Need a Supplement?	29
CHOOSING AND ACQUIRING BROOD STOCK	**30**
Health	30
Buying Your Birds	30
The Choice	31

PREPARING BIRDS FOR EXHIBITIONS — 32
Cage Preparation — 32
Exhibition Condition — 33

SCIENCE AND THE ZEBRA FINCH — 36
Colour Leg Rings — 36
Sperm Storage and Mate Guarding — 37
Conclusion — 37

FEDERATION SHOW STANDARD: A CRITIQUE — 38
Show Points — 38
Interpreting the Standard — 38
- *Conformation*
- *Colour Defects on the Show Bench*

AUSTRALIAN COLOUR VARIETIES: THEIR HISTORY AND ORIGINS — 43
Grey (Normal) — 44
Fawn — 46
Marked White — 48
Chestnut-flanked White – *Fawn Form* — 50
Chestnut-flanked White – *Grey Form* — 52
Slate — 54
Beige — 56
Dilute Blue — 58
Silver — 60
Cream — 62
Dark Cream — 64
Cream-backed — 66
Queensland Isabel — 68
White — 70
Pied Grey — 72
Pied Fawn — 73
Grizzle — 74
Yellow-billed — 76
Black-fronted — 78
Black-face — 80
Black-bodied — 82
Red-face — 84
Western Australian Fancy Form (Black-bodied Silver) — 86
Saddle-backed — 88
Charcoal — 89
Fawn Charcoal — 89

COLOURS RECOMMENDED BY THE FEDERATION OF ZEBRA FINCH SOCIETIES OF AUSTRALIA — 90 - 91

REFERENCES — 92

ABOUT THE AUTHORS

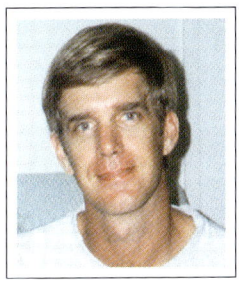

Milton Lewis

Milton Lewis was born into birds, and from a very early age has had a strong fascination and interest in all aspects of aviculture and ornithology, from breeding and exhibiting finches and canaries to making the study of birds his life's work. The science behind birds is what drives him, and is a major reason for the comprehensive nature of this book. A PhD study on the breeding biology and ecology of the Golden-headed Cisticola *Cisticola exilis* in Townsville, Queensland followed by his current position as Senior Wildlife Officer for the Gouldian Finch Recovery Project for the Parks and Wildlife Commission in Katherine, Northern Territory has seen this interest (or should we say passion?) continue. The keeping of finches at home (wherever that is at the time) plays a large role in Milton's life, and has been passed on to him from his father, with whom he used to keep, breed and exhibit caged birds before leaving home to pursue his career in science.

Milton's family support him in his endeavours, and have even been known to get up at the crack of dawn with him, drive many kilometres over rough bush tracks, and help band birds before declaring, yet again, that this will not happen again!

John Lewis

John Lewis has been involved with birds for a great part of his life including many years working voluntarily as a bird bander with John McKean of the CSIRO. While doing this he observed large numbers of Zebra Finches throughout Australia. He was president of the Canberra Bird Fanciers Society for some years before he was presented with life membership. He was a tireless worker when it came to organising annual exhibitions.

John has bred and exhibited Zebra Finches for many years. He counts as his most memorable effort in Zebra Finch showing, the award of Champion Old Zebra Finch at the *Nationals* in Newcastle, New South Wales, but feels his greatest breeding achievements were with Marked Whites during the early 1980s. His first birds of this variety were obtained many years earlier when he purchased two birds from David Burnett of Sydney, New South Wales in 1959. One was a Normal cock, the other a White hen with fawn markings. He paired these two birds and three years later bred the Marked White mutation. This was the beginning of his fascination with the variety. Through a series of perhaps fortuitous events he then obtained Marked Whites from Bruce Read and Harold Fryer, and then several excellent cocks from a breeder in Tamworth, New South Wales. Some of these cocks were bred with Marked White hens, but the most success was obtained when the cocks were bred with Grey hens from Mr Rod Ordish of Canberra, ACT. Later, this line was combined with a stylish Black-face cock from Gordon Coulter. Cocks and hens from this strain won major awards throughout New South Wales, but sadly, the line was lost in 1994 when the birds were stolen from his aviaries. Even with this setback, John has continued to pursue the breeding of Zebra Finches and in particular Marked Whites. At the same time he breeds, exhibits and judges several varieties of canaries, foreign and Australian finches and parrots.

Joan Lewis

Joan Lewis has been painting birds since the early 1960s. Her first attempt, at the request of her husband John, was of an unusual hybrid finch purchased in Melbourne. During the next 20 years Joan taught herself to paint Australian birds with the encouragement of her family and long time friend John McKean. She was later introduced to Dr Richard Schodde and Ian Mason at the CSIRO Division of Wildlife and Ecology. Both these people provided valuable criticism of her work, resulting in two of her paintings being hung in the Division's gallery.

Joan, in partnership with her husband, has visited numerous bird shows and has acquired a wealth of knowledge which has been of great value to her as a bird artist. In producing the paintings for the Zebra Finch they have spent many hours travelling throughout Australia and visiting other enthusiasts in the search for as much information as possible on all the Australian colour varieties of this species.

She has exhibited at numerous art shows throughout New South Wales and other states. A recent work depicting Kookaburras received an award at the Shoalhaven Art Exhibition, and many of her paintings have been purchased by both local and overseas devotees of wildlife art.

ACKNOWLEDGEMENTS

During the course of exhibiting and breeding birds, information is gleaned from many sources. It is impossible to thank all those people, but there are a few who stand out amongst the crowd. These are people who, in particular, viewed the breeding of exhibition quality birds from unique perspectives. From the Canary world we would like to acknowledge both Don Swavley and the late Harry Smith for their instruction on conformation and balance. From the Zebra Finch community we thank the late Bruce Read and the late Gordon Coulter. For his ability to present birds in perfect show condition we thank our friend Don Price.

There are numerous people to thank for providing details about the history of various Australian colour forms of Zebra Finch. Special thanks are due to the late Greg Carey for his information on the 'Red Zeb', as was his way of referring to this unique new variety. We also acknowledge the late Rod Pearce, and later his son, Des Pearce who provided invaluable information on the development of the Western Australian Fancy Form. We are also thankful for advice on the same variety from Bill Hepton. The Queensland Isabel information was received with thanks from Ellis Thornley, as was information about the historical background for the Blackface Zebra Finch from Angus Martin. Other important contributions were made by Bruce Hockley, Bruce Whiting and Gilbert Bunn. For many years Roy Pinch kept good accounts about the origins of many varieties, which provided us with a good basis from which to search for further details.

Again there are many people to thank for reviewing our interpretations of the colour standards. Firstly, we would like to thank the various Zebra Finch societies. These include the Lake Macquarie Zebra Finch Society Inc., the South Australian Zebra Finch Club (now disbanded), the Western Australian Zebra Finch Society and the Zebra Finch Society of Australia Inc. Members of these societies who deserve particular mention are Don Price, Bruce Whiting, Ken Glasson, Anthony Stone and Gilbert Bunn.

We also wish to thank the Federation of Zebra Finch Societies Australia for permission to use their valuable Pantone® colour classification. The Federation members are the Lake Macquarie Zebra Finch Society Inc., the Western Australian Zebra Finch Society, the Zebra Finch Society of Australia Inc., the South East Queensland Zebra Finch Society and the Adelaide Zebra Finch Society.

We would like to thank Birds Australia (RAOU) for allowing us to use their distribution data to compile our distribution map. The Tring Museum (Britain) very kindly allowed us to view and measure specimens. Les Stratford, Syd Boyle, Rhonda Payne, Mark Rattenbury and Alan Leverton provided additional photographs. Thanks also to Grant Bastin for providing us with photographic subjects.

We would be remiss if we did not also acknowledge and thank Nigel and Sheryll Steele-Boyce of **ABK Publications** who have given us the opportunity to have our work published.

Last but not least we would like to thank our families for their contributions. Carol Lewis wrote the chapter on health and read numerous versions of the chapters and Donna Lewis provided computer assistance. Over the many years of exhibiting birds, Brett Lewis has also provided assistance by feeding and watering breeding stock during our absence as we travelled the shows.

The publishers would like to thank Dr Danny Brown BVSc (Hons) BSc (Hons) for his assistance with the health section and Russell Kingston for his overview of the text.

G CHAPMAN

INTRODUCTION

When we sat down to begin the task of writing an Australian book about Zebra Finches, we realised the exciting transition phase that we, as breeders and connoisseurs of this active little bird, are now entering. Times have certainly changed since we first became serious about breeding champions for the show bench!

My (Milton) first real encounter with Zebra Finches came when helping a very close friend, Greg Carey (Uncle Greg). He and a number of other people had decided to establish a Zebra Finch Society in Yass (a small country town in New South Wales), and to start the ball rolling were going to have their first specialist Zebra Finch show. My father (John) and I, for some reason, did not actually own *any* 'zebs' at the time, although dad had certainly owned many before. Anyway, to show our support for friends and birds, we visited a couple of local pet shops the day before the show and managed to obtain six reasonable looking birds. We took them along to the show the next day and to our amazement won Champion Pied Hen with what was actually a very nice Fawn Pied.

Zebra Finch keeping was not our main interest in those days, but we always had a few in the aviary after that initial exhibition. Being of a scientific bent myself, I was more interested in the genetics of the species and the mechanics behind breeding different colours. We were particularly interested in the Marked White mutation as it presented unique problems both through being sex-linked, and because it seemed that previous breeders had unwittingly lost some of the variety's appeal when they bred out the black markings. To this day we are still trying to improve these attributes!

A visit to Sydney, New South Wales for a Canary show always included a side trip to pet shops for new stock and it was then that my interest in Zebra Finches became stronger. That trip we purchased two exceptional Black-face cock birds. It came to pass that these birds were from Gordon Coulter's stock, an aviculturist with an exceptional ability for breeding high quality caged birds of many varieties. These birds formed the foundation of the stock we still breed with today.

That was about 20 years ago and today the Zebra Finch scene is vastly different. Today's Zebra Finch breeders and keepers are much more aware of the genetics involved and how new colours and types can occur. We now officially recognise a whole new range of pure colour mutations and crosses of these mutations to form even more colours. In the early days some of these 'new' colours were tossed out as culls; they did not conform to the recognised standard of the time. We now realise that these little birds have a vast range of colours that can and should be recognised and we are more aware of the genetics involved and how to use them in selective breeding.

This book is about Australian Zebra Finches kept under Australian conditions, by Australian breeders. Previous publications have been written by Europeans and have little bearing on a bird living in hot and dry, or humid areas. Our terminology is also different and so is the way we keep our birds. We intend to document our personal knowledge and the information gleaned from other breeders about the way we, as Zebra Finch breeders in Australia, have successfully kept and improved the aviary bred Zebra Finch, one of the most popular breeds of birds in captivity today.

Milton & John Lewis

HISTORY AND ECOLOGY

First described by Vieillot in 1817 as *Fringilla guttata*, the Zebra Finch is now referred to scientifically as *Taeniopygia guttata* (Christidis 1987). The first specimens were collected from Timor and thus were not of the Australian subspecies. Australian specimens were first described in 1837 when specimens from New South Wales were mentioned by Gould (Synopsis, Birds of Australia pt. 1 pl. 10, 1837; in Zann 1996).

The Zebra Finch is a grassfinch belonging to the tribe *Poephilini*, which includes other common avicultural species such as the Long-tailed Finch, Black-throated Finch, Masked Finch and Double-barred Finch (Christidis 1987a & b).

Two subspecies of Zebra Finch exist: *T. guttata guttata* (the nominate race) distributed throughout the Lesser Sunda Islands, Indonesia and *T. guttata castanotis* found throughout

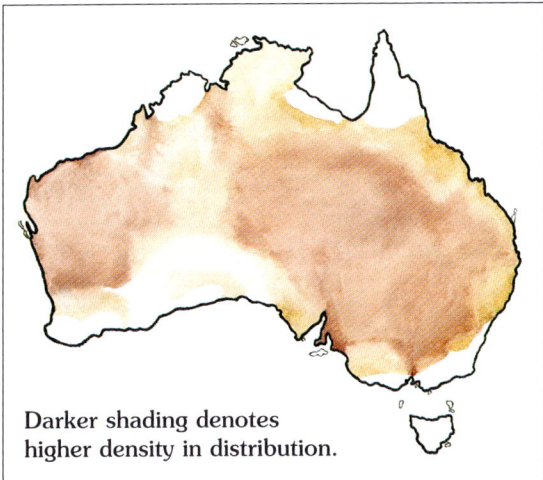

Darker shading denotes higher density in distribution.

Above: Distribution of Zebra Finches in Australia.
Below: Specimens from the Tring Museum of both subspecies of Zebra Finch.

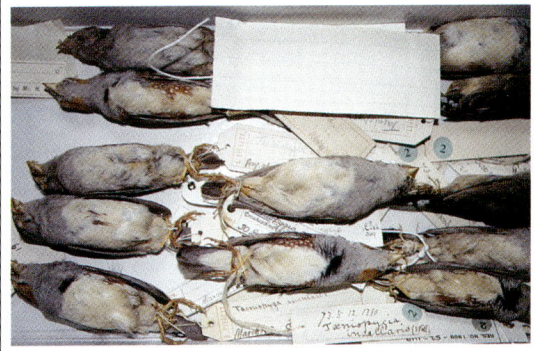

Australia. Although the latter species ranges over most of Australia, its distribution is restricted to drier regions and not the moister fringes of the south-east, south-west, Cape York or the eastern and western coasts of the Northern Territory.

Zebra Finches belong to a group of finches known as estrildidae and are believed to be African in origin (Zann 1996). The genus *Taeniopygia* which also contains the Double-barred Finch exhibits the most primitive characters of *Poephilini* and therefore probably resembles more closely the archetype from which other grassfinches evolved (Christidis 1987b). Although it is impossible to provide concrete evidence for the sequence of radiations leading to the Australian grassfinches we now see, it has been postulated that the initial radiation started in north Western Australia via an ocean crossing from the Lesser Sunda Islands. From this point populations spread across northern Australia and along the eastern coast, where a series of geographical barriers later isolated populations, leading to speciation (Schodde 1982). The timing for these events is also difficult to estimate reliably, but Keast (1981) considers that the ancestral estrildid finches reached the Australian continent 1.5–5 million years ago, during the Pliocene epoch. This also corresponds to a period when the Sahul Shelf (carrying Australia and New Guinea) had come to within 800km of the Sunda plate, facilitating the movement of avian species via the Lesser Sundas archipelago into northern Australia.

Description of the Wild Zebra Finch

The attractiveness of the Zebra Finch has undoubtedly been one of the factors leading to its extraordinary popularity with aviculturists throughout the world. Cocks and hens are quite different in plumage (being sexually dimorphic) with the cock the brighter of the pair.

Comparison of cock (left) and hen face markings in wild Australian subspecies *T. g. castanotis*.

Comparison between cocks of the Australian *T. g. castanotis (above)* and Timor *T. g. guttata* (below) subspecies.

The wild forms *T. g. guttata* and *T. g. castanotis* occur as two subspecies, which are in most respects identical. Cocks have a number of markings that are not normally exhibited by hens. The cock's ear coverts are a rich ochre brown, the flanks are a similar colour with rows of fine white spots and the throat has fine black barring ending in a thick black chest bar. In *T. g. castanotis* (Australian subspecies) the chest bars are on a **white background** whereas in *T. g. guttata* (Timor subspecies) the chest bars are on a **grey background** (Goodwin 1982). The exact ground colour of the chest for the Zebra Finch cock in the current Australian show standard is at present contentious and is discussed at greater length in the chapter dealing with exhibition quality. Cocks and hens have a black teardrop extending from just beneath the eye down over the cheek, a white rump and black tail with white bars.

How Zebra Finches Live in the Wild

In the wild, Zebra Finches are 98% granivorous and feed on a wide variety of both native and introduced seed species (Zann & Straw 1984). Their choice of seed seems largely dependent upon seasonal availability but a trend showing a preference for smaller seeds has been noted. In northern Victoria the main grass species fed upon were Barnyard Grass *Echinochloa crusgalli* (consumed during March to October), Common Wallaby Grass *Danthonia caespitosa* (November to April) and Swamp Wallaby Grass *Amphibromus neesi* (November to January). The two latter species are both native to Australia and fortunately for Zebra Finches, also highly valued as pasture plants by wool growers. All seeds are consumed whole after removing the husks except on rare occasions when larger seeds such as wheat and oats are eaten. Most seeds are taken from the ground although half-ripe seeds are occasionally taken directly from the grass stems.

Large feeding flocks of up to 300 individuals are observed during the non-breeding season of May to August in southern Australian populations (Zann 1996). In populations around Townsville, Queensland flocks of several hundred birds are observed towards the end of the dry season (late spring). This activity is brief, lasting only about a month (October or November, depending on seasonal rain) after which birds appear to disperse and commence breeding (pers. obs. MJL).

Zann and Straw (1984) describe two different feeding behaviours of birds while in a flock, which are dependent upon the type of vegetation they are in at the time. The first is smooth and gradual, with birds along the leading edge of the group gradually progressing forward and being followed by the rest of the flock. This behaviour is usually displayed in open grassy sites. The second feeding behaviour is jerky and erratic and has been termed 'roller feeding'. In this manoeuvre, rolling waves of birds from the rear of the group take the lead positions causing the flock to continually progress forward. This is more often seen in areas of long grass.

Foraging tends to follow a pattern of feeding very early in the morning for a few hours and then again in the late afternoon for three to four hours. During the middle of the day Zebra Finches form small groups and roost in trees near the foraging grounds. While resting they will court and sing, as well as preen. This pattern tends to occur during the entire year with only minor shifts in feeding duration depending on weather conditions or if nestlings are being raised. On cold days feeding bouts are longer and during the breeding season, birds return to their nests after feeding.

Wild Zebra Finch cock.

Breeding in Victorian populations was observed to begin slowly in September, peak the following April and then finish in June. Peaks in breeding were clearly correlated with flushes of growth in seeding grasses (Zann 1996). Zebra Finches appear to prefer breeding as colonies with as many as 47 nests being observed within a single colony at the same time. Nests are usually built in prickly bushes such as *Hakea* species or introduced species such as African boxthorn. Birds have also been observed building nests within Chinese apple and African acacia, both of which are also introduced prickly species (per. obs. MJL). When travelling along the Birdsville track several years ago, we sighted large colonies (20–30 nests) along watercourses. In most cases these creeks were dry, although presumably water was available within the vicinity. All of these nests were built within hollow branches of *Eucalyptus* species and many of the trees were occupied by more than one pair of finches. A curious observation at the time, was that three of the ten nests investigated also held aggregations of large, hairy caterpillars which would undoubtedly have caused skin irritation if we had attempted to retrieve the nestlings from within the cavity. Possibly, this could provide some nest defence if the Zebra Finches were also aware of the caterpillar's defence mechanisms. Zann (1996) mentions similar instances where nests were located adjacent to wasp colonies or within large raptor nests, both of which may afford protection for nestlings. Nests are built both for raising young during the breeding season, and for roosting at other times. Nests used as roosting places are generally simpler in construction than those used for breeding (Zann 1996, pers. obs. MJL). They are all constructed from grass of varying thicknesses. If nesting material is plentiful, the outer shell is formed using heavy stems, often from species of grass with flat, broadleaf blades. The inner chamber, where the eggs are held, is usually formed from finer grasses and may be lined with feathers, fine plant fibres or even sheep wool. On rare occasions nests have also contained pieces of cloth and discarded paper (pers. obs. MJL).

Hens usually begin egg laying before the nest is complete. Clutch sizes can vary, but the normal egg number is five, although I have had several hens produce more than 10 eggs per clutch. The small white eggs take between 12–15 days to hatch but incubation duration appears to depend on the attentiveness of individual pairs (Zann 1996). In wild colonies hens have been found to renest both after successful rearing of a clutch, or following nest predation; however, not all pairs will renest with only 25% producing a second clutch and 20% attempting more than two clutches (Zann 1994).

Both sexes perform all parental duties at the nest (incubation, brooding and nest defence), with hens providing a significantly greater proportion of the duties than cocks (Zann 1996). Both parents actively brood the young for extended periods until about day 11 after hatching. After this age parents spend longer periods away from the nest and usually only return to feed the young. Feeding is performed by regurgitating hulled seed and water and most feeding bouts occur during the early morning and late afternoon. Young mostly fledge at around 18 days of age but this varies from periods as short as 16 days up to longer stays in the nest of 22 days (Zann 1996). In general, fledging takes several days with not all young leaving the nest at the same instant.

HOUSING

Zebra Finches can be successfully housed and bred in cabinets or aviaries. For the aviculturist who does not wish to concentrate on specialist breeding of specific colours, an aviary (large or small) will be suitable. Breeding specific varieties or exhibition birds may require the use of cabinets, one pair per compartment. In this chapter we will describe designs and materials for aviary construction and how to begin breeding Zebra Finches. The designs are either adapted from the aviaries of other aviculturists we have visited or from our own ingenuity through trial and error. After we have covered the general construction of cages, we will then deal with methods of providing clean, safe food and water.

Cabinets

We use timber cabinets for both selective breeding, and housing surplus birds prior to disposal. Cabinets are constructed mostly from 17mm or 19mm plywood, but cheaper pine chipboard can be used if cost is a concern. If chipboard is used, extra care must be given to sealing the timber

Timber breeding cabinets. with good quality paint. This prevents early deterioration of the cabinet due to swelling through the inevitable spills of water during everyday use. If using oil-based paints, you should consider using a paint hardener or tyrolene to reduce the likelihood of birds ingesting small flakes of paint. There is little likelihood that modern paints contain lead but this should also be checked. If the paint does contain lead, do not use it on the interior surfaces of the cabinet because of the high risk of poisoning birds.

A single cabinet usually consists of eight or ten individual compartments, each of which can be used to hold a single breeding pair. This arrangement also allows for a sliding divider between adjacent compartments to be removed, opening up space to fly groups of non-breeding birds. Dimensions of compartments depend on both available space and cage-front size. The measurements given here should be considered as the minimum size required for successful breeding. The overwhelming factor governing breeding success is the happiness of the Zebra Finch, and this is revealed by the general good health of your birds. The preferred dimensions for cage-fronts are about 60cm long x 40cm high with a wire spacing of 1cm. Cage-front size governs the height and length of compartments but the depth is up to you; 40cm is the usual depth. It is advisable however, not to make the cabinet deeper than two-thirds of your arm length or you will not be able to catch the birds out of the cage.

Pair of Zebra Finches in a single compartment for controlled breeding.

Aviaries

The overall appearance of an aviary is far more open to the imagination than that of a cabinet. However the flight area should not be made completely from wire and should contain a section in which birds are able to find shelter from the elements. Birds also need to retreat from unwanted harassment by predatory birds and pests such as cats. Australia has many natural predators that are only too willing to try for an easy meal! The native predators that visit will depend on where you live, but they may include the Kookaburra, Pied Currawong, Pied and Grey Butcherbird or any one of a number of raptor species such as goshawks or falcons. Without a sheltered area within the flight you stand to lose at least one precious bird during your career. Snakes are a problem in some regions, but these require special attention and will be addressed later in the chapter.

Above: Authors' birdroom aviary set-up.

Ready-made aviaries can be purchased from local distributors, but may not suit your birds or the area where you need to place your enclosure. If you are not raising exhibition birds, and wish to have a large cage of beautiful birds to admire, then these aviaries may suit you. They have large, open areas where you can view your birds, but may have sharp edges on the joints. Check all joints before placing any birds in the aviary and file or cover any problem areas.

Care should be taken to locate cages where the weather will suit the birds. They need to have morning sun, but be able to get to shelter and shade when the temperature rises. Another important point to remember when building an aviary is to keep bright lights from shining into the aviaries at night or the birds may be startled and fly against the walls, breaking their necks. You may need to provide a shade or awning of some kind if your outside house or street lights shine directly into the enclosure, or if your aviary is at the end of your driveway.

Always keep in mind the number of birds you are likely to keep, their purpose (will the birds be regularly taken to exhibitions?) and how you propose to look after them. These points will determine how your enclosure is constructed and how large it should be. You may need to consider room for expansion later if your hobby becomes 'bigger' and you will also need to be able to easily access your cages and flights for cleaning and feeding. Visit other aviculturists and enlist their help. Some of these people have brilliant ideas for aviary and enclosure designs, and most will be willing to assist in any way they can. Our rule of thumb for calculating aviary space is *one pair of birds per square metre of floor space.*

Above: Alan Leverton's aviary.
Below: Milton Lewis' aviary.

Method of fixing wire netting to steel frame of aviary.

Construction Materials

Aviaries can be constructed from either timber or steel tubing. Choice of materials depends on your building abilities, budget, and whether or not there are termites in your area. We now use steel tubing for all our aviaries because of its structural superiority, lasting quality and aesthetic appeal. Steel tubing of smaller cross-section than timber is required in the construction of an aviary, making it appear less bulky. Steel aviaries require fewer supports over longer expanses.

The heaviest wire mesh (16 gauge) has, through experience, proven to be invaluable in its abilities to repel predators and stray footballs. Mesh size of 5–10mm is recommended, with 5mm preferred for snake protection. The steel mesh can be fixed to the tubing either by lacing with tie wire or self-tapping screws and washers. If timber is used, staples or horseshoe nails are adequate when securing wire.

When constructing the roof, use galvanised sheeting (or Colorbond™) secured with screws to help prevent wind damage, or the roof lifting. Fibro sheeting can be used for internal walls, and either light gauge steel, fibro or timber for the outside. Any of the readily available cladding materials are suitable, your budget being your only limit. You may be required to blend this new structure with existing buildings or sheds on your property, so always check with the local council before commencing building.

Preventing access by vermin must *always* be considered when constructing an aviary. The majority of fanciers face the problem of keeping an aviary free of mice and, occasionally rats. Those people living away from suburbia will come to realise that snakes are also a problem. Mice are adept at gaining entry to places containing seed, but there are a number of materials that mice find difficult to burrow through. The best is sheet metal or concrete containing fine meshed wire. This can be done by placing 16 gauge 12mm wire mesh in the foundation of the aviary floor. An alternative is to add broken glass to the trench before pouring the concrete. Cracks or crevices in the concrete should be avoided as they allow access for rodents. To aid in the prevention of snakes you may need to erect a skirting of sheet metal around the base of the aviary. This skirting will need to be at least 90cm high and in some instances an electric fence will also be required.

Our latest outdoor aviary was built using these ideas and was started with the laying of a concrete foundation 40cm deep, with 10cm above ground level. The steel aviary was constructed in panels with the wire already attached. The panels were then bolted directly to the concrete using dyna bolts, with 30cm high galvanised sheet skirting around the entire lower edge. The sheltered area for this aviary consisted of a Colorbond™ garden shed with a 30cm x 50cm access hole for the birds cut in the centre of one wall about 90cm above ground level. As a further precaution to prevent mice accessing the aviary, there is no adjoining door between the aviary and the shelter. Access to the aviary and shelter is made via two external doors. This means that if mice enter either of the two areas they will not be able to move easily into the other area.

The aviary is insulated to keep the temperature consistent and to make it easier to keep the room warm during colder temperatures. Several materials are suitable. We have used blue Styrofoam™ sheeting, but this is probably the most costly. More economical alternatives are polystyrene sheets (available from retail outlets such as local electrical importers), tar paper or sarking and batts. Batts are the most likely to harbour vermin as they make an ideal nest for rodents. All insulation can be breached by vermin, so you will need to be vigilant. Place a layer of 12mm wire over the rafters before putting your insulation material in the ceiling; this will help prevent pieces falling down, or the birds accessing the insulation material.

The floor of the external flight is soil and has been planted with a variety of hardy, fast growing grass species, and to date has not been infiltrated by unwanted rodents. The shed floor is concrete that has been built up around the edges above the bottom level of the shed walls. This prevents mice entering gaps between the wall and floor. Concrete floors in the feeding and breeding areas are important for maintaining hygiene and preventing rodent invasion.

Aviary Floors

The floors of aviaries can be an important source of parasite transmission and their design should be given careful thought. Three types of floors can be used: concrete, soil, or a suspended wire floor over either of the previous types. Dirt floors are probably the worst choice as they provide ideal reservoirs for parasites. Suspended floors have the potential to be the cleanest if careful attention is given to the removal of faecal build-up from underneath perches and around seed dishes. Bare concrete floors are considered intermediate in cleanliness, but only if kept free of faeces.

Some fanciers often cover concrete floors with sand or sawdust, in the mistaken belief that it improves hygiene. This is in fact incorrect because such coverings tend to be reservoirs for parasites unless regularly cleaned or replaced because these materials hold moisture and promote growth of mould. It is preferable to sweep a dry concrete floor at regular intervals than to have a covering of absorptive material with the idea that it is better for 'soaking-up' faecal material. Aesthetically, a fresh covering of sand or sawdust is pleasing, but if not changed regularly can lead to unnecessary ill health in your valuable breeding stock.

Perches

Perches are usually constructed from timber dowel, which is readily purchased from hardware stores. To assist in exercising the feet of our birds we often use perches of two different diameters (6mm and 9mm) within all enclosures. In aviaries, perches are placed in groups by drilling lengths of 30mm x 10mm timber with holes of the same diameter as the perches. The dowels are then pushed through and glued to form frames that can be either fixed to walls or hung from the ceiling with wire. Be careful when positioning the perches. Do not place them too close together and avoid hanging them directly above other perches, or above food and water containers. Perches can also be made from more natural resources such as small tree limbs or branches, however metal perches are **not suitable**.

Water Vessels

There are many ways of providing water for Zebra Finches. When housing birds in cabinets, small open dishes can be used or they can be trained to drink from bottles similar to those used by canary breeders. This method is simply an inverted 200ml medicine bottle that has been fitted with a salt shaker lid (single hole) and suspended inside the cage. Care must be taken in how the bottle is suspended. A common method is to make a wire sling but it must be tight fitting as it has been known for a bird to slip between the bottle and wire and break a leg or perish. There are commercial drinkers available that can be clipped to the front of the cage. Open dishes are fine, but these must be shallow enough to prevent drowning and still fit through the door. Probably the simplest and safest water dish, which is readily available, is the tray used under plant pots. These are a suitable depth and made from a variety of materials including plastic and terracotta. Terracotta has the added advantage of keeping water cool (through evaporation) during the warmer months. Another cheap and easy method is to use takeaway food containers that have been thoroughly cleaned. Bleach is a good cheap cleaner and available everywhere. Specialty avian cleaners are excellent, but can be difficult to obtain if you live outside the metropolitan area. Whatever receptacle is used it must be easy to clean and accessible to the bird, as well as capable of holding sufficient water to last between regular changes.

Aviaries can also be fitted with reticulated water. If such a watering system is to be included, then careful consideration should be given to plumbing and drainage before the footings are complete.

Water bottle used in cabinets.

Water dish made from plastic container to be hung on the outside of the cabinet in the door space.

A tap outside the area is also a definite advantage! This will save you transporting water or having a hose stretching across your yard permanently. Another aspect to consider is water quality. Rainwater is preferable, however such a luxury is not available to everyone due to some council regulations and covenants.

Nestboxes

Give the birds a choice of nestboxes by providing a greater number than there are pairs of birds. Generally we supply the aviaries with twice the number of nestboxes as there are pairs of birds. Hang them in different areas of the aviary, away from water and feed containers to prevent faeces or nestlings dropping into seed and water. When placing more than one pair in your breeding enclosure, you may see some aggression. This only occurs for a short time as parents protect the nest site.

There are two general designs for nestboxes. The first is often referred to as a half open box and is so named because the front of the box is half open. The second box is probably more common in Australia and is accessed through a small round hole (45mm diameter) in the front of the box. Both boxes are of the same dimensions, approximately 15–18cm long x 12cm wide x 12cm high. A short dowel perch is usually provided at the front of each box. Structures for nesting can also be made from cylinders of wire or cardboard, or even tins and teapots. Zebra Finches will also nest in natural cavities such as small hollow logs, within clumps of tea-tree and paperbark limbs, and will build in these if provided.

Pests

Mites can be found in breeding cabinets, behind feeders and the ends of perches or in the nest. These pests can harm chicks and irritate adults. Sprays such as red Mortein Plus™ or Coopex™ can be used to eradicate these pests. Always read directions very carefully before using toxic insecticides. Carefully check the directions and read all information before purchase as some products are not suitable for birds.

We have also encountered problems with cockroaches and geckoes. Hens were being disturbed while on the nest, and leaving the eggs for too long. Geckoes were caught and relocated where possible, and the backs of the nestboxes, which were inaccessible to the birds, were sprayed with insecticide.

Above left: Nestboxes for breeding Zebra Finches: standard hole opening (left); half open front (right). Left: Hollow logs can also be provided as a nest structure.

In these instances we used residual contact insecticides which had the added benefit of killing ants. These insects are also occasionally a nuisance in aviaries and nests. This method, with regular applications, appears to have been highly effective, as we have not had problems since.

Preventative measures against the invasion of mice have been mentioned within the section dealing with aviary construction. Unfortunately, it is inevitable that anyone keeping birds will face the problem of rodents entering any structures which house birds. The seed that birds spill onto the floor while feeding is probably what initially attracts rodents, but the aviary also contains water and warm shelter. The first line of defence should be to keep the floor clean of seed and keep all seed and water dishes out of 'mouse reach'. If performed regularly cleaning is easy. The birds become acquainted with the activity and are not overly disturbed.

Feed dish located off the ground on pedestal.

Keeping seed dishes out of reach is a little more difficult. The first rule is not to fasten the tray which carries the dishes to a wall. Mice are able to climb brick, timber (painted and unpainted) and fibro. The only surfaces mice appear to have difficulty climbing are smooth, galvanised sheeting and perspex. Apart from suspending feeding vessels, the other option is to place dishes on pedestals.

Another method of control is incorporating the use of 'bait' boxes. These boxes are useful because only the mice have access to the bait. A similar method is to place a small bird cage containing poison in the aviary. Mice easily move through wire with 10mm spacing to feed on the bait but birds do not. This should only be used if the birds' water supply is inaccessible to the stricken mouse, which will become extremely thirsty after eating anti-coagulant type bait and may die in the water dish.

Breeding

Birds you intend to use for breeding can be pair bonded by placing them together in a show box for several weeks. After this period you will see them sleeping together and preening each other. It must be remembered however, that this does not guarantee parentage of the progeny, as hens are still able to select partners from other cocks within the aviary (see Science and the Zebra Finch, page 36). After placing the pairs in the aviary you should expect nesting activity within one or two weeks. Their propensity to begin breeding may be adversely affected if you have placed the birds in a draughty area, or too close to windows, or their breeding condition is poor.

It is often best to place several handfuls of nesting material in the nestbox before the birds begin building, as this appears to speed up the nesting process. The lining for these nests can be: swamp grass, 'blow-away' or umbrella grass, Newcastle grass that has been bruised and broken, and most seeding grasses. Shredded tissues should not be used, as they soil very quickly and retain dampness. String, hemp or any type of twine are also unsuitable because these

Zebra Finch chicks in nest.

Sanitised chicken feathers used as nest lining.

materials have fibres that tend to tangle around legs and can cause injury or death to young in the nest or even to the parent birds. The use of sanitised chicken feathers, which are available from bedding stores, will ensure that you do not introduce mites. The presence of these parasites can destroy young in the nest and irritate the hen.

As mentioned earlier the average clutch size is five eggs with an incubation period of between 12 - 15 days. Young fledge between 16 and 22 days of age.

Sawdust or rice hulls may be used as floor covering in cabinets when breeding, as this provides a warm area when young fall from the nest. If young become cold, hold them in your hands for a few minutes to warm them, then return them to the nest. If you are a smoker, the nicotine on your fingers can cause feather problems or deter the hen from feeding her young or death. Wash your hands thoroughly before touching any birds, or handling any feed and water containers. Do not smoke anywhere near your birds.

Left: Coloured plastic, numbered rings are placed on nestlings for individual identification.
Below: Closed metal rings are placed on the young at about one week of age.

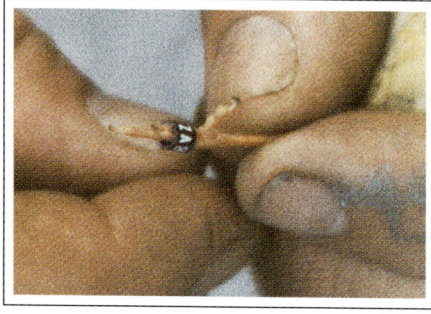

Ringing (Banding)

Many breeders place closed metal rings on the legs of young Zebra Finches before they fledge from the nest. These rings are numbered individually and are also labelled with the year they were purchased. Years are denoted by the colour of the anodising. It is normal practice to obtain a new set of rings each year. Birds bred and rung with the current year's ring can then be shown in 'young' classes during exhibitions the following show season. These rings can be obtained from clubs and must be used if you are exhibiting.

Closed rings are placed on the young at about one week of age. To place the ring on the leg, hold the bird gently in your hand with feet uppermost, slide the ring over the front three toes, up over the back toe and onto the leg. Make sure that the ring slides easily on the leg and that the toes are not caught. Gently return the chick to its nest.

Security

Another important detail to consider with housing, albeit an unsavoury one, is the security of the aviary and your valuable birds. As you will read in other chapters, some lines of Zebra Finch have been all but lost due to the theft of valuable breeding stock. Being able to subsequently identify your own birds if they end up in a pet shop or elsewhere is virtually impossible. Locking your aviary securely, particularly if it is not close to your house, or you have no near neighbours, should be seriously considered. Good quality locks, which are readily available and easy to fit, are essential.

FEEDING

In the wild, Zebra Finches are generalists, feeding on a wide variety of seed. The result is that they are not difficult to feed in captivity and will survive and breed on pre-mixed finch seed which is available from a variety of stores ranging from supermarkets to produce outlets. These mixtures usually contain Hungarian Millet (*Panicum* spp), French White Millet, Red Panicum and canary seed. However, for your birds to reach their full potential we advise that some extra supplements be provided.

Commercial seed mixture used as staple diet for Zebra Finches throughout the year.

Wild Zebra Finches feed during two periods of the day, early morning and late afternoon. Seed is stored in the crop and gizzard and passes through the digestive system in about 87–106 minutes (Cade *et al* 1965). Birds tend to store more food from the afternoon feeding session (600–1000mg) to last them overnight, in the winter months rather than the summer period. The daily energy requirement of a captive Zebra Finch is 35.7 kJ day $^{-1}$ in a non-breeding adult (Lemon 1993). This results in the consumption of approximately 3 grams of seed per day per bird in captivity, and approximately 5 grams per day per bird in the wild (Zann 1996). The digestive efficiency of domesticated Zebra Finches fed on commercial seed is about 88% (Lemon 1993).

Hulled oats.

The following discussion describes the feeding regime we use during both the breeding and non-breeding seasons.

Canary seed.

Breeding Season

The six to eight weeks before and after breeding are possibly the most energetic and demanding time of the year for any birds. If Zebra Finch hens are not provided adequate food prior to egg laying, the result is fewer eggs and smaller young (Haywood *et al* 1992). It has also been demonstrated that if hens experience low levels of nutrition during their first month of life this permanently reduces the size of clutches of eggs. Equally, for a cock to maintain his stamina throughout the breeding season he must be in peak physical condition. To accomplish this we recommend a variety of supplements in addition to the basic finch seed mix.

Rape seed.

Niger seed.

Head study of Normal Zebra Finch fledgling.

To describe the way we feed our birds during this period it is best to outline a typical day's feeding schedule.

The first feed of the morning is an egg and biscuit mix using one of the two recipes given below. This is followed by checking that all the seed dishes are full after the seed husks are blown off. In the middle of the day a small portion of soaked seed is given. This is made by taking the amount of seed required each day for this specific purpose (a small fistful per breeding pair) and soaking it overnight in water. Before feeding this to the birds it is thoroughly washed with copious amounts of fresh water.

The afternoon feed consists of either sprouted seed or green food. Sprouted seed is produced by soaking finch seed mix overnight, washing the seed and draining out excess water. The drained seed is then placed in bottles in which the lids have been replaced by flyscreen netting. The jars are then turned upside down and placed on a windowsill until shoots appear. The sprouts are then washed thoroughly before feeding to the birds. A variety of green food is also available at most local supermarkets but should be thoroughly rinsed before use. The varieties we use include chicory, bok choy, wong bok, choy sum and endive. If available we also supplement their diet with local seeding grasses and milk thistle. Livefood such as

Above: Sprouted seeds which are fed throughout the breeding season.

Right: The varieties of commercially available green foods are wide and often available throughout the year.

Egg and Biscuit Recipes

Ingredients:
1 cup breadcrumbs
1/2 cup crushed arrowroot biscuits
1/2 cup high protein rice cereal
1/2 teaspoon cod liver oil
3 drops wheatgerm oil
OR
1/4 cup chicken layer mash
3/4 cup high protein rice cereal
1 teaspoon Polyaid™
2 tablespoons Wombaroo™ granivore mix
1/2 teaspoon Protexin™ powder

Egg and biscuit supplement which is given as the morning food.

Place ingredients in a bowl and then add one boiled egg, which has been grated or sieved through a mouli, per one cup of dry ingredients. Mix with a fork. (If you try adding dry ingredients to egg, it won't mix as well.)

Each breeding pair of birds receives a small handful each morning with any leftovers discarded.

Left: Mealworms (beetle larvae) are provided when available but generally Zebra Finches prefer only the smaller larvae. Sometimes they will take larger larvae cut in half.

Termites (white ants) are relished by many finch species during the breeding season.

Below: Termite mound.
Below left: Termites.

mealworms and termites are given daily if available but are not considered essential for successfully raising Zebra Finches.

Non-breeding Season

The regular diet of mixed seed is only occasionally supplemented outside the breeding season. During this period we do not feed soaked seed or sprouted seed. Instead we provide a more varied diet of dry seed by including hulled oats, cracked sunflower and cracked safflower in small quantities. Once a week we provide small amounts of egg and biscuit and twice weekly commercially available green foods. Occasionally mealworms or termites are given but this is not part of their regular diet.

Food Storage

Storage of your birds' food is of upmost importance, as disease caused by moisture or mould can wipe out an entire collection. Use drums that prevent insects finding their way into your seed stock and keep them in a dry, cool area. A wide variety of large vessels is available for this purpose including plastic garbage bins or 25 litre drums. To discourage unwanted pests, place a muslin or plastic bag (with holes) filled with bay leaves or garlic inside the drum.

THE HEALTH OF THE ZEBRA FINCH

This chapter provides general advice on the health of your Zebra Finches and how to keep them in their best condition. We have included the basic husbandry techniques and methods that we use to keep our flocks in good health. We have emphasised prevention rather than cure, after finding through experience, that this is by far the best way to care for birds.

The diseases and problems mentioned are those that are most relevant to the Zebra Finch, and medications, treatments and dosages are included, where appropriate. We have chosen not to add prescription only medications to the list, as these should not be obtained or used without the correct advice from an avian veterinarian. We have also laid to rest many old wives' tales regarding the treatment and medicating of birds.

Obviously, if this chapter cannot give you a good idea of what may be wrong with your birds, or does not go into enough depth for you, you may need to consult an avian veterinarian. In researching this chapter, we found the Internet a veritable goldmine of information about up-to-the-minute technology and treatments and about some interesting anecdotal methods as well. We also recommend several important references by Macwhirter 1994, Doneley 1996, and Olsen and Orosz 2000. Full details of these publications are provided in the reference section at the back of the book.

A Few Simple Rules

Maintaining the good health of your Zebra Finches should be relatively simple, and depends almost exclusively on your general husbandry techniques. Preventative medicine is the preferred and most successful method for dealing with health issues. Zebra Finches are a hardy, healthy species of bird, and do not suffer from as many ailments as some of their less robust cousins, such as the Gouldian Finch *Erythrura gouldiae*. If you maintain good hygiene, correct diet and *watch* your birds, you should not be troubled by illnesses in your flock.

Proprietary medicines for worming and minor ailments are available from veterinary clinics, reputable pet shops and larger produce stores. Be aware that it is often cheaper in the long run to take a faecal sample to your local avian veterinarian for examination rather than work your way through a whole range of pet shop products trying to find the one that works. If you have any doubt, take the bird to your veterinarian for a complete examination.

The prophylactic (preventative) use of antibiotics is a common practice that should always be discouraged. Giving a bird a needle 'just in case' can lead to resistance to drugs. As with human medicine, the misuse of antibiotics (and other drugs) is creating problems in this area. When administering medications avoid the 'one drop in the bill' technique. It is of no benefit if you do not know the concentration of your product, the correct dosage or which disease you are actually treating.

When new birds arrive at your facility, keep them in a quarantine area for up to 60 days (minimum of 45 days). Intestinal parasites, among other diseases, have life cycles or pre-patent periods ranging from two to four weeks or more. Some diseases can take longer to manifest, but constant vigilance and stringent hygiene will prevent a significant proportion of these. Your avian veterinarian can test for these diseases and recommend the best treatment to use during the quarantine period.

Observing correct quarantine procedures is a very serious issue which was brought home to us recently. We acquired some Gouldian Finches for a research project and isolated them in quarantine for approximately 30 days (because we were a little short of time). After placing them in an aviary with other Gouldian Finches they started to become ill and were eventually diagnosed with viral hepatitis. Some of these birds are still unwell 12 months later. Luckily these birds were not placed into the aviary with the majority of the population, so the disease did not spread through the whole flock. Most aviculturists will have had at least one disaster with a contagious disease, so be aware and take all precautions to prevent it in *your* birds.

If you have a bird that is genuinely ill, follow any instructions given to you by your veterinarian, and administer the full course of drugs at the correct dose prescribed for the medication. Misuse of medication by increasing or decreasing the dose rate or frequency of a drug can cause problems.

Read the labelling on any over-the-counter product you wish to use, and make certain that it is suitable for birds. If you are not sure, look for a consumer telephone number on the product label and contact the manufacturer. Any good product should have this information available on the packaging somewhere. Alternatively, call your local veterinary clinic and ask the staff for help. They may have contact numbers for the company that are not listed on the product.

Some diseases are zoonotic (transmissible to humans), and this should always be kept in mind when handling your birds. Examples of zoonotic diseases are Psittacosis (*Chlamydia psittaci*) and salmonella. Diseases such as Psittacosis are quite widespread, and many aviculturists today may prove positive to an antigen test. For these reasons, practices such as kissing birds and handling them close to your face should be discouraged.

Good Husbandry Techniques

The most effective way to keep your birds healthy is to use preventative measures that begin with clean food and water.

- **Wash your hands!** Have somewhere to wash your hands before, during, and after handling your birds, particularly if you are a smoker. Antibacterial handwash (available from supermarkets) is recommended.
- **Do not smoke** around the birds or in the aviary. Nicotine can be fatal to birds. The birds can ingest the nicotine from your fingers, inhale it as you breathe on them, or pick it up from your clothes if you are handling them. If you are a smoker, always wash your hands thoroughly or wear surgical gloves when handling your birds.
- **Fresh water is essential**. This does not mean that *all* water dishes need to be changed *every* day. The water may be fine for two or three days, depending on the climate where you live. Stale, dirty water is a good medium for bacterial and algal growth, which can cause illness in your birds. Have a duplicate set of dishes and clean them with a bleach solution. Avoid putting water in metal dishes (except stainless steel), as this may expose your birds to other toxins. You will need to change the dishes more frequently if water is placed in direct sunlight, as algae will grow very quickly in these conditions.
- **Always take your own water** with you when exhibiting or showing your birds. By doing this you can avoid unknown contaminants such as *Giardia*, from other water supplies.
- If you have an outdoor aviary, place a sprinkler or garden misting system inside or just outside the wire. This will provide your birds with a great place to bathe and preen, which will help keep their feathers in good condition and keep your plants green and healthy. This method helps prevent heat stress during periods of extreme temperatures, particularly in the warmer northern regions or during those sudden hot spells in the south. We often 'shower' our birds and find it an excellent way to check on individuals that are not seen very often, as all birds will come out to enjoy the water. However, avoid 'showering' your birds in cold or damp weather.
- **Plant some large pots with local grasses** and place them inside your aviary. This will provide a ready source of fresh, green seeding grass and give your aviary a more natural look. Pots can be rotated or replaced when necessary. You may even find that some of your Zebra Finches will decide to nest in the grass!
- **Provide all food (seed, greens) in containers that are regularly cleaned.** Do not place the dishes underneath any perches or roosts or throw the food on the floor, as contamination with faeces will quickly result. Green food can be pegged to the side of the cage or aviary.
- If you have outside enclosures, ensure that wild birds landing on the wire cannot defecate in the feed or water dishes. It is better to have these containers within a sheltered area rather than in the outside wired section of the aviary.
- The sleeping quarters for your Zebra Finches should be draught-free and dry. Zebra Finches can become ill very quickly if kept in draughty, damp conditions. If you have an aviary that is open on all sides, enclose a corner away from the prevailing winds and rain (see Housing, page 11).
- Try to maintain a rodent-free enclosure. This will be a difficult task, but worth the vigilance if you wish to have a flock of healthy finches. Rats will take birds from cabinets and leave no evidence such as feathers or carcass remains. You will notice the problem only when you discover fewer birds in your cabinet than the last time you checked. Mice will contaminate feed

and water with their urine and droppings and will disturb nesting birds and sometimes eat eggs or chicks. Make sure your feed is stored in sealed containers that are rodent-proof. Nesting material that you have collected for next season should also be kept away from rodents.
- **Check the wire** and make sure that there are no gaps and spaces where birds may get legs, wings or rings caught. This distressing problem is often discovered after finding a bird hanging by its foot. It is not always necessary to destroy these damaged birds, as they can live quite happily with one leg. Obviously they cannot be exhibited but may still be used as breeders after recovering from an injury.

How Do You Know if Your Birds are Unwell?

There are a few easy and inexpensive measures you can take before seeking further advice.
- Take some time to sit and observe your birds for a while, preferably from a location where they cannot see you.
  Watch them feeding and ask yourself whether they are *really* eating, or just sitting in their feed dishes. Check whether they are *actually* drinking, or just *appearing* to do so.
  Are the eyes bright and clear of discharge or are they glazed and weepy?
  Is one bird keeping to itself and not interacting with the others?
- Check the colour and consistency of the droppings – has anything changed? If you watch your birds regularly you will know when something is abnormal. If you are worried, a sample can be collected for examination.
- Do the birds look fluffed-up? Before jumping to conclusions take note of the weather. Perhaps there has been a cold snap and your room is too cool. The birds may be cold and huddling together for warmth. Hang a thermometer in your birdroom for easy reference. An individual bird that is 'fluffed-up' whilst the others are tight feathered indicates a bird with a problem. Refer to Housing, page 11, for building techniques that help keep birdroom temperatures more constant.
- Perform a physical examination. The body should be well covered. A bony keel may indicate that a bird has not been eating, assimilating food correctly, or has a possible disease problem and is therefore losing weight. Birds will use stored energy in the breast muscles to stay alive. Weight loss is not a specific clinical sign and will not allow you to diagnose a specific disease.
- Take a sample of droppings from the bottom of the cage and have it checked for intestinal parasites. This is a relatively inexpensive method to determine if parasites are present. Obtain a suitable treatment immediately.
- Check your feed storage area and make sure that it is not mouldy or damp. Mouldy feed can contain aflatoxins, a deadly form of fungal toxin.
- Check for rodents in your feed storage and the cages. Look for holes in the ground in the aviary, and other signs of their presence. These signs may include faeces in the seeds or along window ledges, dirty marks in cage corners where the rodents are climbing and most importantly, odour. The presence of mice will be quickly detected by the pungent smell of their urine.

If you take these precautions they will assist in preventing most major health problems and significantly reduce the incidence of major outbreaks. Taking the time to actually observe your birds has many benefits, one of which is the simple pleasure of watching and enjoying these beautiful little creatures going about their daily business. This is why you have them in the first place, isn't it?

Zoonosis

The concern of zoonosis is a very real one and should always be kept in mind as you handle your birds or any other animal. There are many diseases that can be transferred from birds to humans, and vice versa. Keeping strict hygiene protocols will help to minimise this substantially. Following quarantine procedures will also reduce the incidence of zoonosis. Many aviculturists may be unaware of diseases to be cautious about, or perhaps they have always known that *something* makes them ill occasionally without actually ever knowing what it was.

Psittacosis (Chlamydiosis, Ornithosis)

Psittacosis is a disease caused by the organism *Chlamydia psittaci*. In finches, it may cause chronic respiratory disease, general ill thrift or may result in reduced breeding performance.

Transmission of *Chlamydia* organisms is via particles shed in feather dust, faeces and discharges from the nose and eyes. Birds may also be carriers while exhibiting no sign of disease. The incubation period for this disease is as little as 12-24 hours, or the organism may remain dormant for as long as seven years in Budgerigars. Infective material can survive outside the body for several weeks.

The incidence of Psittacosis is reported to be approximately 70% in some species of birds in Australia and higher in some Asian countries. For this reason treat this disease with great respect and be cautious when handling birds. The actual incidence of clinical disease in finches is low (estimated to be <5%) but it is still important to be aware of the disease. Wearing facial masks when inside bird facilities, particularly when they are being cleaned, can certainly reduce the risk of contracting this disease. Any infected facilities must be thoroughly cleaned and disinfected fortnightly with benzalkonium chloride, quaternary ammonium compounds, halogenated tertiary amines (eg Avisafe™), or hydrogen peroxide while treating birds with this disease. Cleaners that contain bleach are not effective.

Doxycycline or Enrofloxacin medications are required. These should only be obtained from your veterinarian after correct diagnosis, or may be recommended to use where there are high risk factors. Contact your veterinarian immediately, if you suspect the presence of Psittacosis in your flock. An early diagnosis will ensure that treatment can begin as soon as possible. Birds that recover have no future immunity to the disease and can become fully infected again later. This also applies to humans.

What to Do if a Bird Dies

The integrity of the flock is paramount, and a single bird must not jeopardise the health of the rest of the flock. The wrong diagnosis can result in the loss of an entire flock, and this can happen if untrained people try to treat major outbreaks of disease without knowing what is *really* wrong with their birds.

Even if there are no other sick or dead birds within an aviary it can be worth having an autopsy performed to try and diagnose the cause of the illness. The veterinarian will need to know in advance if possible so that a pathology collection can be arranged. The dead bird should be wet down using soapy water, wrapped in damp newspaper and placed in the *refrigerator,* **not the freezer** as close to the time of death as possible. Frozen specimens are unsuitable as many cells are destroyed during the freeze-thaw cycle, making it almost impossible to determine the state of the bird at the time of death.

The specimen should be as 'fresh' as possible. It may be wise to expend the life of a bird in order to save others in the flock. This is done by leaving a live ill bird with the veterinarian, who will euthanase it at the appropriate time, thus allowing the pathology laboratory to gain maximum use of fresh tissue for post-mortem examination and histopathology. A dead bird kept at home in the refrigerator for more than a day will have gross tissue changes that can give a misleading answer or no diagnosis at all.

Do not underestimate the value of autopsy for diagnosis. Sometimes it is the only way to determine the cause of death and disease in a flock because birds are expert at *not* showing any symptoms until the later stages of their disease.

Worming Program

There are many different types of worming preparations on the market today. Your choice will depend on your location and the type of parasites common to your area. A regular worming schedule will ensure that your birds are as worm-free as possible. Birds with heavy worm burdens are not as healthy, may not breed and will continue to contaminate their environment and the other birds. This can produce an aviary of birds that just do not look as good as they should, and may be susceptible to other diseases because they are immune compromised.

Always worm any new birds during quarantine and before releasing them into your aviary. This should be done at least once, preferably twice. Alternatively, worm your birds on the basis of results of faecal tests by your avian veterinarian. When worming birds in an aviary, a medication given in water is the easiest method of treatment. However be careful in hot weather as birds may overdose on the medication by drinking more than usual. Offer the medicated water for a shorter period each day during hot weather, or wait a few days for the temperatures to drop.

Remove all water containers except the one with the medication and clean out the bottom of the cages or cabinets before returning fresh water in cleaned containers. This will remove all expelled worms and eggs.

Use only glass, plastic or glazed earthenware (the best, but most costly) water containers. Grocery wholesalers sell packs of plastic take-away food containers quite cheaply – these are excellent as they can be re-used for some months and then discarded and replaced.

Care of Sick Birds

Always wash your hands before and after handling sick birds. Sick birds will have a lower immunity to other pathogens, so you do not want to transfer anything to or from the already compromised Zebra Finch. Sick birds need to be kept in a dry, draught-free area that can be kept quiet, and darkened if necessary. Hospital cages and heated boxes are an ideal way of doing this. It is recommended to isolate any unwell birds until diagnosis and any necessary medications are administered. This preventative measure can save a whole flock if the disease is particularly virulent or contagious. The hospital cage should be small, able to be kept warm or heated, and be easily accessed by hand. Hospital cages should be kept away from the rest of the population, preferably not in the same building as the rest of your cabinets or aviaries.

When you have sick birds in 'hospital' make sure you feed them and clean them and their area last. If you attend to sick birds before attending to healthy ones, you may contaminate your whole facility. Personal hygiene is vital.

Any prescribed medication must be given at the correct dose rate and for the full course. Giving a larger dose to 'make the bird better quicker' may not work, may cause toxicities and may be a waste of money. If you do not administer the full course, you are encouraging growth of bacteria that may become resistant to that particular drug.

If using injections, make sure that needles and syringes are sterile. These are available for a very small cost from your veterinarian. Your hands and equipment **must** be clean before injecting. Using blunt, dirty needles can introduce bacteria that are worse than those for which you are treating the bird and will cause pain. Injections should be given into the breast muscle, and if giving daily injections alternate sides so that bruising and pain are minimised. Yes, birds *do* feel pain, so avoid blunt needles and rough handling of ill birds. Your avian veterinarian can teach you the appropriate technique.

The practice of using a particular treatment because it cured the birds in another aviary is dangerous. Unless your birds have been diagnosed with the same disease you should not waste your time and money. This practice leads to the frequent claims that particular drugs no longer 'work'. There are a number of reasons for this:

The wrong treatment was given due to incorrect diagnosis.
The incorrect dose was given.
The treatment was not given for the correct length of time.
The organism may be resistant to the drug used.

Treat only a known disease, and do not make assumptions without some reasonable knowledge of bird diseases.

Respiratory Disease

Respiratory disease is usually noticed when birds are found sneezing, panting, wheezing or fluffed up. There are many causes of respiratory disease including bacterial air sac infections, Psittacosis and air sac mites. All of these will show similar clinical signs and your avian vet will be needed to assist you in determining the actual cause of the problem. Hospital care is important for birds with respiratory disease as these birds are very stressed and may die as a result of their problem if left for too long in the aviary. A quiet, warm, humid hospital cage provides a safe holding facility. It is often assumed that air sac mite is present and treatment (e.g Scatt™) may assist some birds. Quite commonly, these birds may have secondary bacterial infections of the areas damaged by the mites. Your avian vet may implement a treatment regime to treat both diseases together.

Diarrhoea

Diarrhoea or 'scours' are relatively common in all finch species. It may be caused by bacterial organisms, fungal organisms, intestinal parasites (worms or protozoa) or nutritional changes.

Bacterial diarrhoea may occur commonly as a result of stress (and subsequent depression of the immune system) or ingestion of inappropriate bacterial organisms (e.g. soiled water, spoiled foods). Poor hygeine may result in both stress and increased bacterial exposure. Bacterial diarrhoea most commonly causes illness and death as a result of severe dehydration, not necessarily by intestinal damage. Maintaining fluid intake is important for this reason. Your avian vet will need to determine the best antibiotic to stop the diarrhoea. The use of over the counter antibiotics may not benefit the bird and may complicate later treatment options.

Crop and intestinal fungal infections causing diarrhoea are most often seen in younger birds but may affect all ages. *Candida* sp., a yeast, is a very common organism that often develops into inappropriate populations in finches under poor hygiene conditions. It causes diarrhoea as a result of interfering with digestion and often results in larger volume and paler droppings. Another organism that may cause large, pale droppings is Megabacteria. This organism's life cycle and life history is still poorly understood. It is thought that it causes disease by interfering with food digestion at the level of the proventriculus (true stomach). At this stage, only one drug (amphotericin B) seems to treat this disease with any success. It is easily diagnosed from faecal samples by your avian vet.

Intestinal parasites are a common cause of diarrhoea in finches and the most common parasites found are worms and protozoa. The worm types frequently occurring in Zebra Finches are Gizzardworms (*Acuaria* sp.), Threadworms (*Capillaria* sp.) and Tapeworms. Gizzardworms and Tapeworms have an indirect life cycle. This means that the adult worms live in the birds, and the egg stage is taken up by another host (usually an insect or earthworm). This host must then be eaten by another bird to complete the life cycle. Threadworms have a direct life cycle from bird to bird and no other host is involved.

Routine faecal examinations can identify if worms are present and specifically which type of worm is present. This allows for an efficient use of wormers. Worms may be kept out of your collection initially by correct quarantine techniques and appropriate worming at this point. If worms with an indirect life cycle are identified in your aviary, spraying the insect population will reduce reinfection by destroying the worm reservoir. Some suitable wormers for finches include Ivomec™, Wormout Gel™, Panacur™, Droncit™ or Systamex™. Your avian vet can recommend an appropriate product and dose for your individual situation.

Protozoan parasites of importance to finches include *Cochlosoma*, *Giardia* and *Coccidia*. *Cochlosoma* and *Giardia* are from the group known as flagellate protozoa and can cause diarrhoea as a result of interfering with intestinal digestion. They are best diagnosed by microscopic examination of fresh, still warm droppings. *Cochlosoma* may not cause disease in adult birds but may cause significant chick deaths. Both diseases may be treated successfully with Ronivet™ or Flagyl™ as directed by your avian veterinarian.

Coccidiosis

Coccidia are a group of protozoan parasites that infect many bird species including Zebra Finches. Severe infections will cause death and are usually associated with poor hygiene. Infection occurs through direct transfer of parasite eggs from bird to bird in faecal matter. Heavy infections result in intestinal damage with the destruction of intestinal epithelium (lining), which may induce malabsorption, anaemia and hypoproteinemia (protein loss from the gut). Early stages of infection can be observed, eg bloody diarrhoea, but complete diagnosis must be made using faecal flotation which is normally performed by an avian veterinarian. Drugs that are effective against coccidiosis include Amprolium (Coccivet™ and Baycox™), which are given in the drinking water at the manufacturer's recommended dose. Sulphonamides such as Sulpha D™ are also effective in reducing the symptoms of coccidiosis but may not stop losses in severe infections.

In some situations, sudden overfeeding of green food may produce mild diarrhoea as a result of its higher moisture content. Feeding greens regularly and in smaller quantities may prevent this.

Scaly-face (Scaly-leg)

Scaly-face is a mite (*Cnemidocoptes* sp.) and usually appears around the face, although it can also affect the legs. It looks like white flaky crusts or lumps. Scaly-face can block the bird's nostrils and build up around the eye region, so it must be treated as soon as you see it. The mite is easy to kill and treatment is simple. Moxidectin is currently the best available drug and the convenient skin application form Scatt™ is recommended. You may also use dilute Dettol™ and water to the ratio 1:9 and paint the solution on with a brush or cottonbud or apply Ilium Ear Drops™ twice weekly to the affected area. Another method is to smear Vaseline™ or paraffin oil over the scaly areas to smother the mite. Using oil will soften the skin and allow you to remove the dead mites and skin easily with a cottonbud. Try not to put any oil on the feathers because it will affect flight and preening.

Zebra Finch affected with Scaly-face.

Lice and Mites

Many birds are infested with external parasites such as lice and mites. These can be seen as white or black specks on feathers or as missing pieces of feather. Mites come in a number of colours and can also be found on the legs and face. There are many treatments and preventative medicines available, so choose carefully as some medications only treat lice and not mites.

A heavy burden of lice or mites will reduce the ability of your birds to spend time singing or looking for a mate; they will be too busy trying to preen all those parasites off their feathers (Lewis, unpublished manuscript).

Pyrethrin-based products such as Fidos™ Rinse Concentrate or Avian Mite and Lice Spray™ (Vetafarm) are very effective, with a reasonable residual period. Any household insecticidal sprays should be viewed with great caution. Lice live entirely on the bird so spraying the affected birds will treat the problem. Mites live in the environment and move onto the bird to feed. You must therefore spray the aviary and fittings as well, eg Coopex™ or A.I.L.™ (Vetafarm).

Feather Plucking

This will generally occur if there are too many birds in the enclosure. Removal of some individuals will generally result in an improvement. Other causes may be a deficiency in the diet or a heavy burden of lice.

Toxins and Poisons

Growing your own green food and vegetables will prevent insecticides being fed to your birds. Most yards have some space that can be converted into a vegetable garden. Wash any greens and vegetables very carefully before feeding them to your birds. Avoid feeding rhubarb leaves, avocado or green potatoes.

Lead paint is a major concern in areas where older homes are now undergoing renovation. The sanding and repainting of old homes has been responsible for many animal (and human) cases of lead poisoning. If you or a neighbour are sanding and painting, place plastic sheeting around the side of your aviary closest to the work and remove all water and food dishes to a safer area within your aviary. Try to avoid sanding in windy weather. Symptoms of lead poisoning include signs such as paralysis, falling over, convulsions and vomiting. Treatment is with Calsenate™ injections, which will form non-toxic, water-soluble complexes that can be excreted rapidly in the urine and bile. Early diagnosis will mean saving more of your birds. Only your veterinarian can administer treatment. Similar toxicity can occur with zinc injested from galvanised wire surfaces.

Aflatoxins are the most toxic of the fungal toxins and are usually found on mouldy grains and bread. They cause major liver upset, which in turn affects the whole body. It can be fatal and has killed much larger species such as dogs. Any suspect seed or greens should be immediately removed and destroyed. Treatment can be a combination of activated charcoal, steroids or antibiotics. This is definitely a case for your veterinarian to treat.

Eye Injury and Infections

Either of these can cause blindness and birds should be isolated while under treatment to minimise stress. Eye medications usually need to be administered several times per day, so the bird must be readily accessible. Different sorts of injury may need different types of medication. Using the wrong medication may cause some problems eg eye ulcers or much worse. Consult your avian veterinarian for eye problems as you do not get second chances with eyes. Some eye diseases such as conjunctivitis can be transmitted to humans and other birds. When wiping infected eyes, use a clean cotton ball for each 'wipe' so that you do not spread the problem. Wash your hands thoroughly before and after handling infected birds. As with birds with one leg, a bird that has lost its eye due to injury can still feed and breed, so a good cock or hen need not be euthanased if semi-blindness is caused by trauma.

Fractures

Fractures can be caused by the bird flying into something when frightened, by being caught in wire, or by falling. Some fractures can be splinted, with the bird being kept in a small cage while healing takes place. More serious fractures of joints, or multiple wing breaks will necessitate euthanasia. Fibre entanglement (eg cotton wool around toes) will need similar treatment. As mentioned earlier, birds with damaged legs and wings can still breed, and need not be euthanased. For best results, these problems need to be addressed early.

Do My Birds Need a Supplement?

This is an issue that produces many different points of view. From our perspective, the only period your birds should require a supplement is in a time of stress when recovering from illness, when suffering from trauma or during the breeding season. If you feed your birds correctly and maintain good hygiene and husbandry techniques, the need for supplements should be minimised.

Egg food (see Feeding, page 19) is an excellent supplement to give during breeding, and when a bird is recovering from an illness or trauma. The food provides extra protein and vitamins in a fairly concentrated form. Our egg food is prepared in large batches and frozen in small zip lock plastic bags. This will eliminate the problem of the food 'going off' and means that we always have a ready supply for emergencies. Obviously if you have a number of aviaries and breeding pairs, you may need to make fresh quantities of egg food daily.

For birds that have been treated with antibiotics or have had heavy worm burdens, adding a probiotic such as Probotic™ or Protexin™ will be of great benefit. A probiotic contains many strains of 'beneficial' gut bacteria that can help counteract the gut stripping effects of antibiotics and other medications. When Protexin™ was administered to our Gouldian Finches there was a huge increase in brood numbers and individuals reared.

Polyaid™ is a wonderful product that many wildlife carers swear by for bringing birds back from the brink of death. It is an emergency supplement that is high in energy and protein, highly concentrated and quickly absorbed. Giving this to a bird that appears to be quite ill or lifeless can make a huge difference. A bird stressed by being caught in the wire may also benefit from this product.

As you can see, keeping your Zebra Finches healthy is fairly easy, as long as you maintain good hygiene and management principles. By following the basics outlined here, you should have many years of happy, healthy Zebra Finch keeping and breeding.

CHOOSING AND ACQUIRING BROOD STOCK

Choosing or suggesting the ideal bird for someone else is an impossible task. However, it is possible to make suggestions that may lead to the selection of suitable stock to start either a show strain, or a pleasing range of colours for the backyard aviary. It is our intention in this chapter to pass on some established guidelines that we have learnt through experience.

Health

Whether it is for the show bench or the home aviary there is no point starting with sick birds. Zebra Finches are a naturally bright, busy species and if they are not exhibiting this, think very carefully about purchasing them. Do not buy a bird that is sitting fluffed-up in the back of a cage; chances are it will not live very long.

The Zebra Finch you purchase should have a bright red bill, legs and feet (hens are slightly duller in colour than cocks). There should be no scaly white patches on the bill or around the eyes as these are possibly mite infestations. Do not buy birds that are not clean around the vent, as diarrhoea is indicative of several illnesses. If possible,

Black-face Zebra Finch hen.

physically examine the condition of the bird. Healthy birds are rounded in the hand and have plenty of muscle development around the breast, and the keel or breastbone should not be prominent.

During your perusal of prospective stock you will occasionally notice birds with laboured breathing. These individuals could be suffering from one of a variety of ailments which may range from a slight chill to pneumonia, and in most cases these birds will probably die within a day or two of your taking them home.

Before making a final selection, endeavour to observe the birds from a distance. When scrutinised at close quarters, a sick bird will often give the impression of a tight-feathered, healthy bird and will only fluff up when it is viewed from a distance.

If still unsure about the health of the birds, one should keep in mind that the ultimate responsibility for the purchase of the birds is with the buyer. If in doubt, go without!

Black-face Zebra Finch cock.

Buying Your Birds

Deciding where to purchase your birds is really a matter of personal choice and in our view, does not make a lot of difference as long as they are healthy. If you buy stock from pet shops or breeders who cannot provide the breeding history, then you can only expect what you see; there is no way of knowing the pedigree of the bird. These birds could contain recessive genes so that when you breed with them they could produce a variety of different colours.

This is fine if you want to produce Pieds or Fawns. However, if you are a purist and wish to produce only Greys *from* Greys, it may be a problem. On the other hand, if you purchase birds from a reputable breeder then you at least have the chance of knowing the breeding behind the stock.

There are a number of methods for contacting Zebra Finch breeders. If you live in a capital city there will be local avicultural societies and in some instances, even specialist Zebra Finch societies. These clubs are usually listed in the Yellow Pages™ under 'Clubs and Societies'. The other way to find local breeders is to ask at your nearest pet shop; sometimes they will give you a name and telephone number.

When choosing stock for the show bench, life immediately becomes more difficult! Novices will find this very hard in the beginning but after the few initial mistakes we *all* make, it becomes progressively easier. The following words of advice are not meant as a hard and fast rule for buying reasonable birds, but a method based on personal experience and a few mental calculations.

If you intend to start with Zebra Finches of exhibition quality there are two things we recommend that you do. Firstly, you should contact a local or state Zebra Finch society to find out when the next show is and to obtain a few newsletters and past show results. After carefully reading the results of several shows (the more the better!) you should expect to have a reasonable idea of the exhibitors who are currently breeding stock of reasonable quality in the colours you want. With this knowledge you should then start to contact those people and enquire about the availability of purchasing a few pairs.

Marked White Zebra Finch cock.

As a general rule we have found it far more useful to purchase pairs than single birds. This is because it is often best to keep different bloodlines together until you understand what progeny are being produced. Sometimes crossing bloodlines can produce spectacularly good show birds, but more often than not it produces little of value. Once you have purchased several pairs it is time to start breeding! Try not to be in too much of a hurry; you may need to wait until the end of next breeding season to buy the birds you want, if the breeder does not have surplus stock for sale.

The Choice

What happens if you are confronted with the wonderful situation of having to choose your breeding stock from a box containing 20–30 Zebra Finches? Possibly the best course of action is to be systematic and keep a clear picture in your mind of what you want. Carefully look for closed rings on the birds' legs, as these will tell you the age of the birds. Young birds can be considered at face value because not even the breeder will have test mated these birds yet. Sometimes it is best to be careful about buying older birds; older birds may have already been used and are being sold for a variety of reasons. Sometimes they are poor feeders of nestlings, produce low quality young for the show bench or, in rare cases, may be so obnoxious that they cannot be easily housed with other finches. However, you must remember that the older birds must also have had good points worthy of consideration, otherwise they would not have been kept for breeding the previous season. Next, keep in mind the varieties you *really* want, and don't be caught out by the dazzle when faced with the array of so many wonderful colours. Buy what you *need*!

PREPARING BIRDS FOR EXHIBITIONS

Exhibiting Zebra Finches is a common pastime throughout most of Australia and the rest of the world. These events are often held on weekends and are usually single day events. Exhibitions range in size, but may contain from as few as 100–200 birds to over 1000 birds. These birds compete for prizes and ribbons. Exhibitors begin several weeks beforehand with the preparation of show cages, birds and entry forms. Schedules for exhibitions can be obtained from the show secretaries of Zebra Finch societies and contain a list of classes. Each colour variety will have classes separating individuals by both sex and age. Instructions on how to enter are usually presented within the schedule.

Cage Preparation

Zebra Finches are exhibited in standard cages that are painted white inside and black outside. All exhibitors use identical cages to set a level playing field where only the bird is judged and not the exhibitor or cage. Personal identification marks are not allowed anywhere on the cage as this constitutes a

Right: Benched exhibits at a Zebra Finch show.

After the exhibits have been judged they are presented with their prizes and ribbons.

Page 32

Standard Zebra Finch show cage used when exhibiting in New South Wales.

marked cage and can cause exclusion from a club or disqualification of that exhibit. The only identifying feature allowed on the cage is a sticker that is placed on the bottom left-hand corner and supplied by the show secretary. The sticker contains information about the class in which the bird is entered.

The show cages must be clean and freshly painted at least once a season, however, if they are used often, then more frequent repainting may be required. It is a good idea to complete the painting several weeks ahead to allow the paint time to dry and harden before birds are introduced. On more than one occasion we have seen exhibits in freshly painted cages where the bird has also received a dab to the tail or wings because the paint was not quite dry.

Plain yellow millet is generally the accepted seed, and shell grit the floor covering used in show cages. However, this can vary depending on the requirements of different clubs. It is best to check the show schedule for these details. Seed and shell grit should be carefully placed in the cage using a funnel. Shell grit and seed pushed through the front of the cage by hand could damage the paint and leave dust and dirt on the front holding bar.

A standard plastic drinker is fitted inside the cage on the third bar from the door (this applies to New South Wales finch clubs, and may not apply in other states).

Utmost care should be taken in providing clean, tight-fitting, level perches. Loose perches will cause birds to be unsteady in the cage. Scraping a hacksaw blade along the wood grain can roughen perches. This will help the bird grip the perch. Do not overdo this, as little pieces of wood and splinters will cause bleeding and irritation to the feet. Perches are generally cleaned with bleach. This both disinfects and whitens the wood.

Exhibition Condition

There are myriads of practices devised for conditioning birds before exhibitions. Let's just say that the simplest is probably the best. Assuming that the birds have comfortable housing, with a high quality diet there will be very few problems. Training birds to show is a procedure where birds are quietened, and is necessary in order to have the birds present themselves at their best. Scared, agitated individuals perform poorly on the most part because judges are unable to view them at their best. Birds caught out of a big aviary are harder to train than birds that are bred in cabinets. This is inevitable, as cabinet birds are more familiar with being in small cages from the day they hatch, while aviary housed birds are not used to confinement.

After choosing our birds for exhibition, we

Seed and shellgrit show cage funnel.

Show cages in carry box before transportation.

generally start the training process by keeping them for several weeks in a double breeding cabinet. We then divide the area in half with a wooden slide before introducing individuals to the show cage. Their first experiences in show cages are generally limited to short periods of 30 minutes, but this time is lengthened to a full day (the equivalent of an exhibition) over the course of one or two weeks. During this training period we also play music to simulate the noises heard at exhibitions.

While the birds are in their training show cages, we occasionally spray them with a fine mist from an atomiser containing water. Spraying with water is generally thought to improve feather condition through improved cleanliness and through increasing the time birds spend preening. Another training method is to have a show cage placed at the end of the cabinet so that the bird can freely travel from the cabinet into the show cage. This reduces the need to handle the birds before a show and therefore minimises stress and the possibility of damaging feathers.

Training birds for competition may also require more than simply allowing the birds to become accustomed to the smaller show cage. The following remedies may help in some situations but are generally considered unnecessary for most birds.

The first situation may occur after birds have gone through the initial quietening period. In rare instances an individual may prefer to sit on the bottom of the cage instead of the perch. This can be solved by placing tinfoil, shiny paper, or water on the floor of the show cage during training. Apparently, the slippery or noisy surface forces the bird to stay on the perch where it becomes accustomed to staying even after the foil is removed.

Another problem is a bird which crouches while sitting on the perch. This can sometimes be remedied by attaching a piece of cardboard to the front of the cage above perch level so that the bird must stretch to look over the top.

When your birds are finally ready for the show be careful during the transportation. We prefer to place our birds in their show cages the night before and keep them in a quiet corner of the bird room, or packed in the car if it is an early morning departure. When carrying your birds to and from the car or around the show always hold the cages front to front in pairs to minimise disturbance. Do not leave the cages on the floor, cage front facing out where people walking past will disturb them and most importantly provide them with clean drinking water throughout the day.

G CHAPMAN

SCIENCE AND THE ZEBRA FINCH

The Zebra Finch could probably be described as the avian equivalent of the white laboratory mouse. In the study of evolutionary ecology Zebra Finches have been used to investigate the way mate choice occurs. This has led to a variety of papers dealing with many aspects of competition among mates by both cocks and hens, and the attributes used by individuals to select mates. This chapter seeks to help Zebra Finch enthusiasts by offering some interesting ideas about mate selection not previously mentioned in any other avicultural texts.

Colour Leg Rings

It is a common procedure for both aviculturists and avian researchers to place brightly coloured plastic rings on the legs of birds to facilitate individual identification. When doing this, we have in the past given absolutely no thought to the possibility that this practice may be influencing the behaviour of our birds. After reading the following paragraphs your view may well change. One of the most memorable papers about Zebra Finches was published by Nancy Burley in 1985 and was followed up by others (Burley 1986, Burley *et al* 1982). These papers explored the theory and provided data showing that hen preference for mates could be manipulated with the application of certain colours of plastic leg bands. It was found that the behaviour of hens could be altered, and that the sex ratio of nestlings could also be changed.

Nancy and her co-workers found that Zebra Finch hens preferred to mate with cocks that had red leg bands. Cocks however, did not find this colour at all attractive on hens, instead preferring black bands on their partners. In the other extreme it was found that cocks wearing a light green band were least preferred by hens, and hens with a light blue band were unattractive to cocks. If birds were banded with orange rings their sexual status remained unchanged. At first these findings may appear a little far-fetched and difficult to believe but Burley *et al* (1982) explained the preferences in relation to the plumage of cocks and hens. In the case of hen preference for red, we should consider the bill colour of cocks. Zebra Finch cocks have a bright red bill, in fact much brighter than those of hens. The difference in bill colour between the two sexes would suggest that this character is sexually selected and could be used in hen mate choice. It is reasonable, therefore, to predict that the addition of extra red may increase a cock's attractiveness. On the other hand a cock would not necessarily prefer a more masculine hen so the addition of red to a hen may in fact reduce her attractiveness. This was indeed found to be the case. Black was shown to increase a hen's attractiveness and in wild hens this is the colour of the hen body marks. This leads us to postulate that perhaps the hens with black chest bars that we are currently rejecting on the show bench are in fact the sexier hens from a Zebra Finch cock's perspective. The finding that light blue or light green bands were unattractive is not unreasonable since neither of these colours occur in the body colour or markings of Zebra Finches.

In a separate paper Burley *et al* (1986b) went on to show that colour bands could also influence the sex ratio of nestlings. Zebra Finches will sometimes reduce their brood. This is done by either starving some nestlings or by simply removing nestlings. It is thought that brood reduction is most often practised during periods of low food availability. Burley *et al* (1986b) postulated that chicks were sexed by call and that chicks of the same sex as the less attractive parent were starved or removed. Roper (1993) has found recently that differences in call pattern do exist between the sexes, but there are no sex specific calls used by nestlings. Zann (1996) appears to treat this data with some reservation, preferring to wait until more field evidence is available, but the idea does deserve some thought. If you have been trying to breed hens from a particular pair and have been unsuccessful, why not try giving the hen a black leg band and take the red band off the cock!

Following this work Swaddle *et al* (1994) found that not only were some colours 'sexier' but the placement of the bands also had an effect. If bands were used in a symmetrical order (orange/green on left leg + orange/green on right leg) cocks were preferred as mates against those of non-symmetrical placement (green/green on left leg + orange/orange on right leg). The logic is linked to an evolutionary theory referred to as 'fluctuating asymmetry' (Møller 1990), which postulates that hens or cocks of any species will prefer more symmetrical mates because this indicates genetic quality. There is much conjecture about this theory and our ability to measure appropriate levels of asymmetry. It is an interesting idea and many researchers are still exploring the possibilities.

Burley et al (1994) also found that Zebra Finch hens mated to green banded cocks are more likely to be promiscuous than hens mated to red banded cocks. The cocks they sought matings with were more likely to be from the higher quality red banded birds. There is always some level of infidelity within a large flight of Zebra Finches, so just imagine what could be happening if you have rung your favourite cock with a red band. That could explain why you bred that one really good individual within a nest of mediocre birds.

Sperm Storage and Mate Guarding

Zebra Finch hens are able to store sperm for 10–13 days (Birkhead et al 1989). The sperm is stored in specialised tubules located at the junction of the uterus and vagina (Birkhead 1987). Not all sperm from each ejaculate are stored within the tubules however, as only about 0.1% (6,027 spermatozoa) are held. The rest of the ejaculate is lost with the passage of faeces. Birkhead et al (1989) determined that eggs are fertilised about 24 hours before being laid and that hens have a fertile receptive period which begins about 11 days before the first egg is laid and ends 24 hours before the last egg is laid. However, once egg laying has commenced the fertilisation window in which spermatozoa are able to reach the infundibulum (without obstruction) where the ovum for the next egg is located prior to shell deposition is only about one hour after the previous egg is laid (Birkhead et al 1993). During this fertile period partners are almost inseparable, with cocks following their hens whenever they go off to feed or drink. This is known as mate guarding and is performed by cocks to reduce the likelihood of unwanted copulations from other cock suitors.

Unfortunately for the Zebra Finch cock, this is also the time of greatest nest building activity. This results in the cock having to make frantic excursions to find nesting material while leaving his mate within the nest. The cock will normally not leave the hen until she is safely within the nest chamber and calls to her for the entire period of his absence.

If hens are seen to have copulated with another cock or have managed to slip past her partner's guard for any period of time he will usually copulate with her immediately upon her return. This is known as a retaliatory copulation and in the first instance will reduce the chance of the previous cock fathering any young by about 50%. If the social cock copulates a second time within four hours of the first extra-pair copulation the chance of the outside cock being a father of any young is reduced by 80%. The phenomenon where the last cock to copulate with the hen increases his chance of fathering her young is known as last cock precedence (Birkhead and Møller 1992).

Conclusion

What this all means to the aviculturist is that Zebra Finch hens have a variety of mechanisms for mate choice. They can spend over a week of time before egg laying, copulating with cocks and storing sperm before the first egg is produced but they can also mate each morning after they lay the first, second and third eggs. They participate in sperm competition, where hens mate with a variety of cocks prior to egg laying. All of these cocks have the potential to father young within the same clutch depending on the viability of their sperm. However, if a hen is seen by her social mate to have copulated with another cock, or she has been absent too long, then her mate will effect retaliatory copulation with her. This copulation effectively flushes out the sperm of the previous cock, increasing the likelihood of her social mate being the father of her young (last cock precedence). In addition to this their colour rings can alter the attractiveness of an individual. This certainly leaves us a lot to think about after we release several pairs into a breeding enclosure. Perhaps our breeding records are not as accurate as we thought.

FEDERATION SHOW STANDARD: A CRITIQUE

In this chapter we intend to briefly introduce the standard Zebra Finch as it is recognised by the Federation of Zebra Finch Societies, Australia (1995). Specific descriptions of colours are presented in the next chapter, but here we provide a broad view of the exhibition point system, a critique of the standard and the general faults observed in show specimens.

Show Points

Zebra Finches, like most other caged birds, are exhibited competitively for both prizes and prestige. There are a large number of regional shows at which Zebra Finches and other varieties of caged birds can be exhibited, as well as specialist society shows and the national exhibition at which both individual exhibitors and state teams compete.

Birds are judged against each other, based on a point score system and a description of an imaginary bird of perfection. The description of perfection as well as diagrams displaying angles of position and body shape can be obtained from local Zebra Finch societies. An illustration of a generalised ideal exhibition Zebra Finch is not included because all of the colour illustrations depicting each variety have been based on the recommended 'type' (See Australian Colour Varieties: Their History and Origins, page 43).

At this point it is worth defining what 'type' actually means. In the Standard this term refers to the general shape of a bird. If a bird is of good type it closely resembles the ideal specimen described within the Standard. Type will include characters such as head shape and size, and body proportions such as wing length or bill size.

Points allocated to areas of importance in exhibition Zebra Finches are as follows:-

Type	40
Markings	25
Colour	15
Condition	15
Size	5
Total	100

Interpreting the Standard

Conformation

The consistent breeding of high quality exhibition Zebra Finches requires a solid understanding of all aspects of the Standard. It is not merely a case of being lucky (although this always helps), or looking at the picture and trying to replicate the image in the real bird. If there is one point to be held above all others, it is that in order for a bird to perform well on the show bench it must be comfortable. To achieve this, the bird should be balanced and in proportion. Judging if a bird is balanced is often subjective but a more technical understanding can be obtained by considering where the centre of gravity lies on the side view of the bird. For a bird to be balanced in the perched position the body's centre of gravity should lie directly over the top of the feet. Legs should be held slightly angled and not horizontal. Some breeders consider short legs an important component when choosing stock, probably because shorter legs position the body of the bird closer to the correct centre of gravity and thus improve the **impression** of balance. When correct balance is achieved, the bird will sit at approximately 30 degrees to the horizontal. This is measured by imagining a line drawn from the tip of the bill through to the tip of the tail. The tail should finish level with the perch.

In keeping with the perception of balance, careful note should be taken of the position and shape of the head. The head should be broad, round and also have depth of back skull. Although not a common fault, some birds tend to be 'browy', that is having pronounced eyebrow ridges. These birds appear as though they are frowning and should be avoided when exhibiting.

A more common problem is the positioning of the head; too far back onto the shoulders and the head position shifts the centre of gravity back, causing the bird to sit more upright and forcing the legs into a horizontal position. The second problem resulting from poor head carriage is the

Common type faults in exhibition Zebra Finches.
a) correct type, b) incorrect position of head too far back on shoulders, c) too much back skull, d) incorrect dropped tail and small head.

disruption of a gentle, even edge along the back. In birds where the head is too far back the drop from the back of the skull to the back of the body is too steep. Some breeders describe this as a 'teapot' shape.

Wing carriage and wing shapes are also important in the overall quality of exhibition birds. Wings should sit close to the body, not appearing as if they have been glued on as an afterthought. Several problems commonly appearing in this area are crossed wings, long secondary feathers and, more rarely, dropped shoulder feathers. The first problem is where the wing tips cross and do not rest adjacent to each other on the rump. The second problem of elongated secondary feathers often manifests itself in the form of messy wings. Long secondary feathers tend to hang down below the primary feathers, destroying the clean lines of the leading edge of the wing. Dropped shoulder feathers are sometimes the result of an injury, but can also be inherited. The feathers in question are more correctly termed alulas and again, distract from what should be an even leading edge to the wing.

Very few serious problems exist with the tail apart from its being carried at the wrong angle. A good tail should be strong (broad for the entire length), have large, even white bars and be well filled underneath with the undertail coverts.

Continuing on from the tail, the underside of the body should form an even rounded sweep past the chest and along the throat to the beak. The area around the breast should not bulge as is often the case with overweight birds.

The beak should be small, compact and functional. A finch bill is engineered to crack the hard outer cases of grass seeds, so selection for exhibition birds should never forget the form and function aspects of the characters that we select to change. One of the truly wonderful features of domestic Zebra Finches is that they still resemble and function like wild Zebra Finches. It would be a shame to lose this appeal through selective breeding in the misguided search for an artificially ideal bird, as has been done in several other varieties of caged birds.

Colour Defects on the Show Bench

Apart from specific problems of incorrect shades of colour for specific varieties of Zebra Finch, there are problems that appear to be genetic.

The first is inconsistency of shading across wing feathers. In particular, the prevalence of brown or fawn edges to the flight feathers of Grey varieties is very common. This is also observed in other varieties such as Fawn, where the edges of some flight feathers have reddish tinges similar to the colour seen on cock cheek lobes. It is important to note that this colour fault is totally unrelated to the blotchy colour sometimes seen in the wings of Fawn Zebra Finches, which is often the result of bleaching. For this reason it is best not to keep exhibition varieties of dilute Zebra Finches in aviaries exposed to direct sunlight.

Another common fault is the presence of white tips on the flight feathers. We have often found this in Grey varieties bred through Marked White and Chestnut-flanked birds. These individuals are valuable as splits in breeding such varieties but are not to be exhibited.

Probably the worst fault that persists amongst newcomers to the show world is wrongly exhibiting Pied birds in non-pied classes. A Pied Zebra Finch is any individual with a white feather in the ground colour, eg. Normal birds with a white feather in the wing, head or tail. It does not matter how large the white feather is; it is still Pied. Some unscrupulous people may remove such a feather for show purposes but if they breed with the bird then they are only

A poor example of an exhibition Pied Zebra Finch with a small number of white feathers.

fooling themselves. The bird will **always** carry the Pied gene and will pass it on to all its offspring and so perpetuate the problem. Incidentally, if you do decide to show it as a Pied, it is unlikely to win because a good Pied should have about 50% of the ground colour in white.

There seems to be controversy amongst some members of Australian Zebra Finch societies regarding the throat colour in Grey varieties, but we suggest that the mistake has arisen because of an optical illusion. In the standard, the zebra stripes on the throat of grey cocks are described as a grey background with an overlay of black stripes. However, the chest feathers of the wild Australian Grey Zebra Finch cock, from which our domesticated stock presumably originated, are white with black edges. The grey basal colour described in the Standard is in fact that found in the Timor subspecies (Zann 1996, pers. obs.).

Upper body of a wild Zebra Finch cock displaying the white, not grey feathers of the chest and the black edges.

The dilemma therefore, is whether the Standard should take into account the wild colour from which domesticated stock originated (Australian subspecies) or use the colour found in the Timor species which, admittedly, was the first described subspecies of Zebra Finches, although rarely kept in captivity. Perhaps the misconception has arisen because large numbers of white feathers with black edges placed over each other (as occurs on the chest) may give an illusion of grey.

Black-face Slate Zebra Finch cock.

AUSTRALIAN COLOUR VARIETIES: THEIR HISTORY AND ORIGINS

In presenting this chapter we have attempted to provide the reader with as much information as possible pertaining directly to varieties of Zebra Finch unique to Australia. These are varieties such as the Slate, Queensland Isabel and Black-fronted. We have, for completeness, included varieties such as the Pied which are found throughout the world, but admit that they are of unknown or dubious origin. The chapter also mentions several varieties, which at the time of writing are not recognised by the Federation of Zebra Finch Societies, but which we still consider worthy of discussion. The information provided includes a brief historical account of each mutation's discovery and breeding, as well as exhibition characteristics approved by the Federation.

Attempting to piece together the historical accounts of colour varieties specifically originating in Australia has been extremely difficult. The passing of information from one generation of Zebra Finch breeder to the next has undoubtedly introduced twists to the stories over which we have no control. Therefore, with this in mind we have attempted to give the best account of how new mutations were discovered and the people involved in bringing these varieties into public view. We apologise if mistakes have been made, but we selected the histories that seemed the most logical and correct, and again gratefully acknowledge all those people who were so willing to help (see Acknowledgements).

At present there are 12 colour forms that are best described as ground colour mutations. These are Grey (Normal), Fawn, White, Marked White, Slate, Beige, Dilute Blue, Silver, Cream, Dark Cream, Cream-backed and Chestnut-flanked. The remaining colours we would like to describe as overlays, because any of these patterns can be found in conjunction with the previously mentioned ground colours. The overlay patterns are Pied, Grizzle, Black-face, Black-fronted, Black-bodied and Yellow-billed. An example of one of the many combinations between ground colours and overlays might be a Black-face Slate. The Western Australian Fancy Form (not a dilute form of the Black-bodied Zebra Finch of the Federation of Zebra Finch Societies), the Red-face and the Charcoal colour varieties are also described and are possibly three new overlay mutations.

In order to standardise the colours of all these varieties, the Federation has chosen to use the Pantone® colour chart to identify the individual tones and hues of each type. We have summarised this information as a quick reference (See page 90-91).

Pantone® Colour Coding

Code	Colour	Code	Colour
1c	Light Silver-grey	465c	Beige
3c	Silver-grey	472c	Pinkish Fawn
10c	Cool Grey	475c	Light Pinkish Fawn
149c	Pale Orange	482c	Cream
155c	Apricot	1525c	Orange-brown
156c	Dark Apricot	1655c	Reddish Orange
172c	Orange	1675c	Reddish Brown
185c	Red	4625c	Dark Brown
404c	Slate	4645c	Fawn
405c	Dark Grey	4665c	Cream
425c	Dark Grey	4675c	Dark Cream
430c	Bluish Grey	4715c	Pinkish Fawn

Above: Grey (Normal) cock.
Below: Grey (Normal) hen.

Grey (Normal)

The first Grey Zebra Finches bred in captivity were from stock captured in the wild. The exact region of Australia where these birds were caught is uncertain (Zann 1996), but many of the first trappers worked the northern regions so it is possible that they came from the Northern Territory or north Western Australia.

Captive Grey Zebra Finches have dark eyes and red beaks (the cock's beak is darker than the hen's). Comparing wild Grey Zebra Finches and domesticated Grey Zebra Finches has brought to light some interesting, and perhaps controversial, observations. It has been noted that most aviary bred stock lack the red iris of wild birds (Sossinka 1970 in Zann 1996). We have checked most of our domesticated stock and found that this is not the case. It may be that domestic Australian stock differs from that used by Sossinka (1970) in Europe. A very interesting comment made by Carr and Zann (1986) was that Australian aviculturists have not selectively bred for body size. We as aviculturists know that this is not the case. We can only presume that the domesticated stock, from which they took their measurements, were culled birds discarded to pet shops, or that their wild stock were larger birds than those available to Australian enthusiasts. There are some other differences between wild Grey birds and the current show stock, for example the back colour is browner in wild birds.

Description

The face area of the Grey Zebra Finch between the beak and the black teardrop is white. Cheek lobes are orange-brown and, from the underside of the beak to the black breast bar, a white throat with black lines. The head, neck and wings are grey, the rump white and the tail coverts black with white bars. Grey cocks have reddish brown side flanks with white spots and underparts are white to buff towards the vent. The legs and feet are orange-red in both sexes. The hen is grey without cock markings, has a reddish orange beak (lighter than the cock) and an off-white rump.

Above: Fawn cock.
Below: Fawn hen.

Fawn

Mr Fred Lewistka of Adelaide, South Australia pioneered this colour variety. He began in 1935 with two light brown or fawn hens given to him by his brother Mick. These birds had been observed huddling around Mick's campfire, 600km north of Adelaide at Coward Springs. These early breeding efforts produced Fawn hens. It was not until some years later that Fawn cocks were produced. The delay was probably because this mutation is sex-linked. Although Fred was only interested in the Fawn mutations, he also produced some very light fawns and odd coloured birds which he called 'Smokies'. These individuals were probably sold, but are now presumed to be the forerunners of the Dilute Blue and Cream. Many of these birds were apparently exported worldwide and resulted in the establishment of the Fawn variety in a number of other countries, including South Africa and Belgium.

Description

Fawn Zebra Finches are a recessive and sex-linked mutation often considered similar to Cinnamon Canaries but differing in that they have dark, not red eyes (Blackwell 1988). As with most of the other varieties they also have a red beak (duller in the hen) and a white facial area between the bill and the teardrop. The throat stripes, teardrop and breast bar are dark brown. The other markings worn by cocks are not diluted, therefore the cheek lobes are orange-brown, and the side flanks are reddish brown with white spots. They should have a fawn upper body (head, neck and wings) with dark brown tail coverts with white bars, and a tail one shade lighter than the coverts. The rump is white and underparts are white to buff towards the vent. Unfortunately, many Fawns have the incorrect colour in this area and are more typically buff over the entire belly. In the hen the cock markings are replaced by fawn, the rump is off-white and the beak is reddish orange.

It is worth noting that many Fawns differ significantly from the Standard by having black teardrops, breast bar and stripes and black tail. It may be that two different mutations exist, a dark and a light form. This has been the case for the Chestnut-flanked mutation in which it is now recognised that a Grey form exists.

Above: Marked White cock.
Below: Marked White hen.

Page 48

Marked White

It appears that the earliest record of the Marked White Zebra Finch can be attributed to Mr Whitehouse, who caught three White hens in Queensland in 1937. After many years of selective breeding he produced White cock birds with similar markings to the Normal Grey. These birds were given the name of Marked White. Years later in 1948, selective line breeding was carried out by Mr Levitt Hunt of Pymble, New South Wales. He also commenced with three pure White hens, their origin unknown. The hens are described as having black teardrops and almost black tail bars. From these birds pure White cocks with normal markings were produced. In 1950 Mr Hunt obtained three hens from Mr Whitehouse. He noted that these birds were not pure white like his own, and after breeding them produced young with off-white bodies and lighter markings. It appeared that he had a Dilute variety. Consequently, it is likely that Mr Hunt's birds were the normal Marked White and Mr Whitehouse's birds were the mutation now referred to as Chestnut-flanked. Another early breeder of around the same period was Mr Howlett. His efforts are noted because his birds were apparently dispersed more often to other breeders, thereby increasing interest in this variety.

Interest then waned until about 1959–1960 when Mr Eric Brown of Sydney, New South Wales produced an outstanding cock. This bird went to Mr Bruce Read where it was mated with Grey birds. Quality improved, numbers increased and by 1970 the Marked White became a popular show bird.

Description

The Marked White Zebra Finch is basically a white bird with normal markings. The cock should have a white head, neck, wings and throat. The upper breast is white with black lines and black breast bar. Facially, cocks have orange-brown cheek lobes and black teardrops similar to Grey cocks. They also have reddish brown side flanks with white spots, black tail coverts with white bars, with the tail two shades lighter than the coverts. Their rump and underparts are white. The hen is similar to the cock except that all cock markings are replaced with white and the beak is reddish orange rather than red. The eyes of both sexes are dark and the feet and legs are orange. The Marked White mutation is recessive and sex-linked.

Above: Chestnut-flanked White - Fawn Form cock.
Below: Chestnut-flanked White - Fawn Form hen.

Chestnut-flanked White
Fawn Form

As mentioned in the section on Marked Whites, the origins of this variety are uncertain, but can probably be ascribed to Mr Whitehouse.

Description

In basic terms, the Chestnut-flanked White - Fawn Form Zebra Finch is a white bird with dilute markings. As with other varieties of Zebra Finch they have dark eyes, a red beak, orange feet and legs. The teardrop is fawn, as are the breast bar and the lines across the throat. The pale orange cheek lobes are reduced in colour intensity if compared to the Grey. The side flanks are pinkish fawn with white spots. Tail coverts are fawn with white bars, and the tail is two shades lighter than the coverts. They have a white rump, underparts, face and head. In the hen all cock markings are replaced with white and the beak is reddish orange. This mutation is recessive and sex-linked.

Above: Chestnut-flanked White - Grey Form cock.
Below: Chestnut-flanked White - Grey Form hen.

Chestnut-flanked White
Grey Form

Unlike the Chestnut-flanked White - Fawn Form described previously, the grey form of this mutation has dark grey teardrops, breast bar and throat stripes, instead of fawn. The tail coverts are also dark grey and the tail is several shades lighter than the coverts. Cocks have pale orange cheek lobes, and pinkish fawn side flanks with white spots. The remainder of the bird (face, head, back, wings, rump) is white. The eyes are dark and feet and legs are orange. Cocks have a red beak, while hens' beaks are reddish orange. Until recently birds fitting this description were often considered to be poor quality Marked Whites and discarded. This mutation is recessive and sex-linked.

Above: Slate cock.
Below: Slate hen.

Slate

In 1960 a finch breeder in Narrabeen, New South Wales discovered the appearance of several 'light grey' birds within her aviary. Mr Bill Plimmer of Dee Why West, New South Wales was asked to look at these unusual birds which exhibited normal cheek patches and side flanks but all the black markings were replaced with dark grey. The birds were passed on to Mr Read who laid the groundwork in reproducing this new mutation, then referred to as the Normal Blue. Various breeders produced many birds during the late 1960s and early 1970s but due to non-acceptance on the show bench, breeders discontinued working with them and the variety quickly began to disappear. In 1978, Mr Geoff Roberts of Glenbrook, New South Wales produced three cock birds. The parents were a Marked White cock and a Grey hen. In previous years Mr Read had bred Slate through his Marked Whites and it was from this line that Mr Roberts bred his Marked Whites. Mr Roberts gave a cock to Mr Read who then produced Slates. These are now a popular variety and available to all breeders.

Description

The Slate Zebra Finch is easily recognised as being different from a Dilute Blue by the evenness of the wing colour. Mr Bruce Read was a visionary when it came to breeding Zebra Finches and we remember that he was the first breeder who brought to our attention the fact that the Slate variety did not have a patchy wing colour.

Typically, Dilute Blues have patchy colour over the wings (although we are of course trying to eliminate this problem). However, Slates show one colour throughout the wings and back. They have a slate head, neck and wings, dark grey teardrop, slate throat and upper breast with dark grey lines and dark grey breast bar. The orange-brown cheek lobes and reddish brown side flanks with white spots are similar in colour to that found in Grey individuals. Tail coverts are dark grey with white bars, and the tail is one shade of grey lighter than the coverts. The Slate hen differs from the cock by the lack of cock markings and has an off-white rump and reddish orange beak.

Above: Beige cock.
Below: Beige hen.

Beige

It appears that the existence of this very recent variety can be attributed to Mr Bruce Whiting. Mr Whiting observed the different colour after combining the Slate and Fawn. Genetically, the colour is interesting in that it combines both sex-linked and recessive factors which in some ways are similar to dominant Creams and Silvers. To illustrate this, suppose a Grey cock (pure, without carrying recessive mutations) is mated to a Beige hen; the resulting young are grey in colour, but the cocks carry (split) Beige, Fawn and Slate and hens carry, or are split for, Slate.

Description

The Beige Zebra Finch differs from other colour varieties in the body colour. The head, neck and wings are beige. Teardrops are light brown, throat and upper breast fawn with light brown lines. The breast bar is light brown. The cheek lobes are orange-brown, and the side flanks are reddish brown with white spots. The face area between the bill and the teardrop is white. They have light brown with white bars on the tail coverts. The rump is white and the underparts are white to buff towards the vent. The hen lacks the cock markings and is completely beige with a reddish orange beak and an off-white rump.

Above: Dilute Blue cock.
Below: Dilute Blue hen.

Dilute Blue

From 1935 onwards Mr Fred Lewistka of Adelaide, South Australia probably bred the first Dilute Blue during his endeavours to produce a Fawn mutation. He produced birds that he called 'smokies' but disposed of them to dealers and overseas, especially Belgium. Some of the birds sent to dealers were obtained by Mr Hunt of Pymble, New South Wales and Mr Jack Wedderburn of Carringbah, New South Wales around 1948–1950. Between them a mutation was established which is now known as Dilute Blue.

Description

The Dilute Blue Zebra Finch has a bluish grey upper body and head. The head of the cock has dark grey teardrops and apricot cheek lobes. The throat and upper breast are bluish grey with dark grey lines, coupled with a dark grey breast bar. The lower body and the rump are white and the side flanks are pinkish fawn with white spots. The tail is two shades lighter than the dark grey tail coverts that also have white bars. The face is white the eyes are dark and feet and legs are orange. The hen has all cock markings replaced with bluish grey, and an off-white rump.

Above: Silver cock.
Below: Silver hen.

Silver

In 1960 Mr C Harris of Parkes, New South Wales produced a very light silvery-coloured hen from a mixed collection of Dilute birds. Through selective breeding he then produced a strain of Silver birds. Mr Doug Simms and Mr Bruce Read obtained several of these birds and bred them so successfully that others were able to obtain breeding stock from them.

Description

The Silver Zebra Finch is light silver-grey over the head, neck and wings. Typically the face has silver-grey teardrops, white cheek lobes, and white between the red beak and silver-grey teardrop. Cocks have a light silver-grey throat and upper breast with silver-grey lines, a silver-grey breast bar, and light pinkish fawn side flanks with white spots. Both cocks and hens have silver-grey tail coverts with white bars, and the tail is two shades lighter than the coverts. Cocks have a white rump, while hens have an off-white rump.

Above: Cream cock.
Below: Cream hen.

Cream

Mr Fred Lewitska might have bred this mutation when producing the Fawn variety. This source is suspected because Mr Lewitska referred to occasional 'light fawns' appearing as he developed Silver and Fawn varieties. Mr Levitt Hunt and Mr Jack Wedderburn both bred with these birds, resulting in a popular mutation now available to all Zebra Finch breeders.

Description

The Cream Zebra Finch has dark eyes, white cheek lobes and white facial area separated by dark cream teardrops. They have a pale cream head, neck and wings, with a cream throat, dark cream upper breast lines and dark cream breast bar. The underparts are white tending towards buff near the vent area. The side flanks are light pinkish fawn with white spots. The tail is two shades lighter than the coverts, which are dark cream with white bars. The cock has a red beak. Hens are the same as cocks in colour but lack the cock sexual markings (throat stripes, cheek lobes, side flanks), have an off-white rump instead of white and a reddish orange beak.

Above: Dark Cream cock.
Below: Dark Cream hen.

Page 64

Dark Cream

The recognition of this variety is relatively new and undoubtedly owes its existence to new insights into Zebra Finch breeding. During earlier periods (15–20 years ago) we considered the Dark Cream an unwanted colour produced when breeding the lighter, more desirable Creams exhibited at the time.

Description

In simple terms this variety is several shades darker on all areas of the body than the Cream. Dark Cream Zebra Finches should have dark eyes, red beak and orange feet and legs as do the other varieties. However, the head, neck and wings are cream, the teardrop and breast bar are fawn, and the throat and upper breast are cream with fawn lines. Unlike Creams, which have white cheek lobes and pinkish fawn side flanks with white spots, the Dark Cream has dark apricot cheek lobes and pinkish fawn side flanks with white spots. They also have fawn tail coverts with white bars, the tail two shades lighter than the coverts, white rump and the underparts are white to buff towards the vent. The hen has cream markings with a reddish orange beak and off-white rump.

Above: Cream-backed cock.
Below: Cream-backed hen.

Cream-backed

Early in the 1960s, Mr Bruce Read and Mr Dennis Glacken discovered what they thought was a Cream hen at Ace Colony bird dealers of Westmead, New South Wales. On noting that the bird had a pure white body, they decided that it might be a Penguin*. Mr Glacken paired the hen with a Normal grey cock. The pair produced hens similar to the mother, and cock birds of similar ground colour to the mother but carrying cock markings in a dilute form. This was not a 'Penguin' but a new mutation, and from there a strain of Cream-backs was established and has become a standard mutation. Another important feature was that unlike Marked White and Chestnut-flanked mutations, the Cream-backed Zebra Finch is recessive but not sex-linked.

Although the Cream-backed mutation has in the past been mistakenly labelled as a poor quality Marked White or 'rubbish' Cream, this variety is both eye-catching and unique. It is typified by high quality fine feather. Good specimens perform well in exhibitions.

Description

They have a dark cream head, neck and wings with a white breast. The teardrop, breast bar and breast stripes are fawn. Cocks have pale orange cheek lobes and pinkish fawn side flanks with white spots. The beak is red, eyes are dark, face is white and feet and legs are orange. The tail coverts are fawn with white bars and the tail is about two shades lighter than the coverts. Unlike the hens of other varieties, Cream-backed hens have dark cream side flanks, a white breast bar and cheek lobes, and an off-white rump. The remainder of the hen's colour is the same as the cock but with a reddish orange beak.

* *The Penguin mutation occurs in European and UK aviaries but does not appear to exist in Australia. Its main features are that cocks do not have breast bars or striping. Hens of this mutation also differ from other varieties by having white cheek patches. Some forms of this mutation also lack facial tears. Genetically, Penguins are recessive and can appear in a variety of colours but the most common are Normal and Fawn. They acquired their name because they superficially resemble a penguin due to the white chest.*

Above: Queensland Isabel cock.
Below: Queensland Isabel hen.

Queensland Isabel

The first specimens of the Queensland Isabel occurred in the aviaries of Mr Bob Knox on the Gold Coast, Queensland and were passed to a breeder Mr Ellis Thornley, who then went on to develop a strain. The first two birds were cocks, and occurred in a flock of Black-bodied Grey birds. The first cock appeared in early 1989, was of poor quality and proved infertile. The second cock appeared in late 1989 and was healthy and very fertile. The second cock was mated with a Normal hen and produced Normal cocks and hens, as well as Fawn hens. These young (splits) were then paired together and the first of the Isabels appeared, with hens showing three shades of cream. The hens of the middle shade, which matched the cocks, were then mated and more Isabels produced. Cocks of both the darker and lighter shades have now been produced and to date the lighter shade resembles the American Florida Fancy. Work is still in progress on the darker shade.

The Isabel Zebra Finch is the newest recognised mutation that has appeared in Australia to date, although more mutations are being looked at, but not yet recognised.

Description

This mutation is basically a Cream-bodied bird, lacking a breast bar, zebra throat stripes and teardrops, and would appear to be similar to the Isabel found in Europe. The breeding characteristics are recessive, as are those of the overseas birds, so the name Isabel has been applied. Although experimental breeding is not complete, this variety appears only in the cream ground colour and not the grey. Young in the nest are recognised by their pinkish bills, whitish pink skin and black eyes.

Unique amongst Zebra Finch mutations in Australia, both sexes of the Isabel Zebra Finch lack teardrops and the cocks are also devoid of the breast bar and throat stripes. Being a Dilute it closely resembles the Cream in colour. The head, neck and wings are cream with the primary (flight) and secondary feathers edged with orange. The creamish grey of the throat and upper breast extends to the bottom of where the breast bar would normally be positioned. Cocks have red beaks, dark orange cheek lobes and reddish brown side flanks with off-white spots. The cream tail coverts have off-white bars, and the tail and rump are light cream with buff underparts. The hen has cream markings with reddish orange beak and an off-white rump.

Above: White cock.
Below: White hen.

White

Apparently Mr A J Woods bred the first Australian examples of pure White Zebra Finches in 1921. These birds (three hens), were purchased by Mr H Lyons who successfully established the variety through selective culling.

Description

The White mutation is recessive and has dark eyes, red beak, pure white body colour (all over) and orange feet and legs. The hen is similar to the cock with a reddish orange beak. It is worth noting that this variety is not an albino and can be recognised as such by the absence of red eyes.

Above: Pied Grey cock.
Below: Pied Grey hen.

Pied

The Pied Zebra Finch is a recessive mutation in which whole feathers are white, replacing the ground colour of other varieties. These white feathers appear at random, but for exhibition standards it is preferred that the individual areas of colour (cheek lobe, breast bar etc.) are 50% replaced by white feathers. The Pied mutation can appear in all ground colours and in all varieties of Zebra Finch.

Above: Pied Fawn cock.
Below: Pied Fawn hen.

Above: Grizzle cock.
Below: Grizzle hen.

Grizzle

In 1959 Mr Bruce Read purchased an oddly coloured Grey hen from Newcastle, New South Wales. As the result of selective breeding he was able to reproduce the colour in both cocks and hens. Body colour was grey, but a 'salt and pepper' effect resulted from each feather carrying a white fleck. The hen carried grey cheek patches.

Mr Read worked on the Grizzle Zebra Finch for some years, improving the type and proving that this bird was not a Pied. The pure Grizzle variety has now almost disappeared from aviculture and the show bench. Very few breeders kept and maintained this bird, and with the deaths of older aviculturists who bred this variety, it may not be seen again. The few specimens that remain probably have Pied through them, and therefore are not the pure strain.

Description

The important quality defining a Grizzle Zebra Finch is that each feather is sprinkled with white specks. This is different from that previously described for Pied birds where whole feathers are white. A feature of note regarding feather colour of the Grizzle is that the 'salt and pepper' effect is not apparent until the bird emerges into its adult plumage. Coloured feathers on young in the nest will therefore identify the nestling as a Pied.

The cheek lobes of cocks are mostly replaced by grey, and in exhibition specimens it is preferred that about 12% of the original lobe colour remain. The overall desired effect is described as 'salt and pepper' over the entire body. As with the Pied Zebra Finch, this variety appears in a variety of ground colours. It is available as Fawn Grizzle, Grey Grizzle and technically, as any other colour.

Above: Yellow-billed cock.
Below: Yellow-billed hen.

Yellow-billed
Description

This variety differs from all other mutations by the colour of the bill. In the cock, the bill is deep orange-yellow. The hen's bill is several shades lighter. The other areas of this variety should conform to the colours described for the other varieties. Feet and legs are yellow and darker in the cock than the hen. For instance, if the Yellow-billed bird in question is Fawn, the body colour should be the same as that of the Fawn, as described. The Yellow-billed Zebra Finch appears to be recessive to all other mutations.

Above: Black-fronted cock.
Below: Black-fronted hen.

Black-fronted

Mr Bruce Read of Cameray, Sydney, New South Wales began breeding what led to the first strains of Black-fronted Zebra Finches early in 1960. He obtained two wild Grey cocks from near Charters Towers, Queensland and mated them with his own Grey hens. These pairs produced some good Greys and a hen with black tail coverts and a slightly black face. He mated the hen with its wild father, producing hens similar to the mother and cock birds with black tail coverts. These young cocks also had black chest bars that extended up the throat to the beak with half the teardrop also extending to the beak.

In the early 1970s very few people participated in specialist Zebra Finch breeding and the Black-fronted was almost lost. Mr Read decided to again take on the challenge and began another breeding program for this mutation. Luckily, Mr Pinch had three Black-fronted birds, two hens and a cock, which he gave to Mr Read. Disastrously, the breeding program was thwarted when the birds were stolen from their enclosure. Fortunately, Mr Read had given several Grey birds bred through Black-fronted birds to Mr Peter Walsh of Booroodoo, near Bowral, New South Wales. These birds eventually produced Black-fronted individuals, two hens and one cock.

The cock and one of the hens were given to Mr Gordon Coulter of Strathfield, New South Wales and the remaining hen to Mr Read. Mr Coulter's birds eventually went to the dealers, but Mr Read went on to breed from his hen, and this produced a number of split birds. The hen died and some of the splits were given away, but Mr Pinch managed to obtain one pair and produced a Black-fronted hen. Later breeding produced both cocks and hens. This mutation appears to be a difficult variety to rear to maturity. However, Mr Pinch has now successfully bred Black-fronted birds in Grey, Fawn, Marked White and Normal Blue (Slate).

Description

Although superficially similar to Black-face and Black-bodied Zebra Finches, the Black-fronted Zebra Finch has only 50% of the area between the bill and beak filled in with the teardrop colour and is devoid of tail bars in both sexes.

Above: Black-face cock.
Below: Black-face hen.

Black-face

Unfortunately, the origin of this variety is clouded by conflicting stories. In an article written for *Australian Aviculture* in 1977, Mr Bill Gordon of Ringwood, Victoria noted that in 1938 in north-west Victoria, he observed a flock of Zebra Finches landing on his grape trellis. An abnormally coloured cock was conspicuous for its large black bar. He believed this to be a Black-face mutation. No mention is made as to how this bird was obtained, or if indeed it became the patriarch of our present Black-face variety.

In a recent conversation with Mr Angus Martin, formerly of Leeton, New South Wales we traced yet another bird that undoubtedly has connections with the current stock of Black-face mutations. It appears that a 'black-barred' bird was sighted at Mr Martin's orchard sometime in the 1950s. Mr Martin spoke about it at a local bird meeting and Mr Eric Piltz became interested. He obtained the bird and placed it in a cage with Normal Grey Zebra Finch hens at Mr Martin's farm. They produced heavier marked cock birds and some hens that had grey cheek patches. The birds may have then gone to Mr Harry Nesbitt, a friend of Mr Piltz.

According to information from Mr R Pinch, Mr Nesbitt caught a cock bird near Leeton, New South Wales in 1959. He failed to reproduce with it, and gave it to Mr Bill Maggs in 1960. Mr Maggs bred successfully with it, producing a Black-face cock and several Greys. Eventual hatchings produced enough birds to reasonably establish the mutation.

An extensive breeding program using pairs of these birds was then carried out by Mr Eric Baxter of Manningham, South Australia. His belief was that three variations existed:

1. Black-face: Normal Grey as caught in the wild with large black bar and black face.
2. Grey-backed Black-face: As above but having dark grey back and wings.
3. Black-bodied Black-face: Similar to the first two variations but with black extending down to the tail and extending further up the chest.

The Black-face is now a common variety exhibited throughout Australia. It can be obtained for most colours, but is still more easily available in the Normal form and Dilute Blue or Silver. Most of the colour varieties are now also available as a Pied Black-face.

Description

This dominant mutation differs from other mutations in that there is a pattern change. It is typified by having the usually white area between the bill and the teardrop replaced by the breast bar colour. In the hen this area is the same colour as the upper body (the Grey hen has grey lores). The breast bar of the cock extends towards the legs.

Above: Black-bodied cock.
Below: Black-bodied hen.

Black-bodied

As mentioned previously, it is assumed that the origin of the Black-bodied mutation is connected to the arrival of the Black-face. Genetically, the Black-bodied resembles the Black-face, both types being dominant.

Description

This variety differs from the Black-face because the colour of the breast bar extends up to the chin and back to the undertail coverts. It is preferred that the side flanks are devoid of white spots, although it could be considered that this may well detract from the striking appearance of this variety. The hen has all cock markings replaced by body colour.

Above: Red-face Normal cock.
Below: Red-face Normal hen.

Red-face

In 1981, Mr Greg Carey of Yass, New South Wales purchased a Black-face Zebra Finch cock from a pet shop in Sydney. He noted that the bird was rather unusual, but at the time was a little perplexed as to why it was different. We (Mr Carey and the authors) later determined that the features which separated it from the usual Black-face variety was the missing teardrop, and the pinkish red (not black) area between the bill and the cheek patch. A Black-face hen and the unusual cock were then released into an aviary along with two other pairs of Black-face mutations.

A number of Black-face Zebra Finches were bred in the cage but Mr Carey was unsure of their parentage. In 1982 he noticed that one young cock had colour similar to the flank colour on his chest. This led to closer scrutiny being conducted until two other young cocks were found also showing brownish red below the bar. Mr Carey then discovered three young hens, one with distinct pink ear patches, another with red feathers on her chest and the third with less distinct ear patches. In early spring of 1983, these hens, as well as the original cock and two young cocks (presumably sons) were released into a large aviary with other Australian and foreign finches.

A few weeks later five young Zebra Finches appeared, two hens and three cocks. Two of the cocks were Grey and the third cock had Grey markings, but his bar was the same colour as his flanks. All the hens produced that year carried pink cheek patches. The cocks carried larger and brighter cheek patches, plus a reddish tinge on the head feathers. Some of the cocks showed red above the bar and down the front.

Sadly, Mr Carey passed away in May 1985 and we knew little about where his Zebra Finches had been sent. We had obtained a pair from Mr Carey in 1984 but experienced poor breeding success. Young were dying in the shell before hatching and several hatchlings suffered from abnormalities such as extra toes. Presumably, this was the result of inbreeding. Mr Carey had also experienced this problem. We then assumed that with such poor breeding results, and not knowing the whereabouts of the rest of Mr Carey's stock, the new variety would be lost. To our relief it now appears that this mutation is alive and well with the recent emergence of several specimens in the aviaries of Ms Rhonda Payne and Mr Mark Rattenbury. At the time of writing, the Federation had yet to recognise a Show Standard for this variety. The authors are hopeful of the inclusion of this unusual mutation in the Standard in the future.

Not a recognised standard at time of publishing.

**Above: Western Australian Fancy Form (Black-bodied Silver) cock.
Below: Western Australian Fancy Form (Black-bodied Silver) hen.**

Western Australian Fancy Form (Black-bodied Silver)

The Western Australian Fancy Form was previously referred to as the Black-bodied Silver Zebra Finch and was bred by Mr Rod Pearce, probably in 1985 in Perth, Western Australia. He acquired Grey Black-face birds from Adelaide, South Australia in the early 1980s, and using selective breeding and cock birds with more black than others, he spent several years bringing the black down from the chest bar and removing the white, until he had the Black-bodied Grey. He then crossed these with Silvers and after several more years produced the Black-bodied Silver. Importantly, these birds are distinctive because unlike Dilute Blue or Silver, or Black-bodied birds, the chest, teardrops and tail coverts are black, not grey (diluted). After a brief experience in breeding this variety ourselves it appears that this form of the Black-bodied variety may well be a new recessive mutation, and quite different from other Black-bodied Zebra Finches seen in the eastern states of Australia. This is certainly a variety with a bright exhibition future and well worth further experimental breeding. There was no set Standard for the Western Australian Fancy Form at the time of writing this book.

Not a recognised standard at time of publishing.

**Above: Saddle-backed cock.
Below: Saddle-backed hen.**

Saddle-backed

This colour pattern does not appear to be derived from a specific mutation but is merely a very white Pied. This is not recognised in the Australian Standard or the British Standard but is within Europe (Blackwell 1988). Basically they are white birds with a saddle-shaped patch of coloured feathers (usually fawn or grey) on the centre of the back.

Not a recognised standard at time of publishing.

Charcoal

A recent colour mutation within Australia the Charcoal has not yet been given recognised standards for exhibition purposes. They appear to be very dark over the entire body, lack tail bars and hens also lack facial tears. At present there has been mention of two colour forms, Normal and Fawn but it is highly possible other forms will appear as the breed becomes more popular.

Its origins as with most other mutations are somewhat shrouded in conjecture. A canary breeder, George Hiscock recalls observing these birds in Gordon Coulter's aviaries as far back as the early 1970s. These birds were ultimately sold to Featherdale Farm where they were acquired by Alan Turner. Other aviculturists have since produced birds thought to be from the original strain. Our observations of this striking mutation were made at the home of Bruce Hockley. He is currently working on a breeding program with this mutation.

Not a recognised standard at time of publishing.

Above: Charcoal cock.
Below: Charcoal hen.

Fawn Charcoal

Fawn Charcoal cock.

Not a recognised standard at time of publishing.

Fawn Charcoal hen.

COLOURS RECOMMENDED BY
THE FEDERATION OF ZEBRA FINCH SOCIETIES OF AUSTRALIA

Colour Variety		Face	Eyes	Beak	Tear-drop	Cheek Lobes	Head, Neck & Wings	Throat & Upper Breast
Grey	Cock	white	dark	185c	black	1525c	10c	10c with black lines
	Hen	white	dark	1655c	black	n/a	10c	10c
Fawn	Cock	white	dark	185c	4625c	1525c	4645c	4645c with 4625c lines
	Hen	white	dark	1655c	4625c	n/a	4645c	4645c
Marked White	Cock	white	dark	185c	black	1525c	white	white with black lines
	Hen	white	dark	1655c	black	n/a	white	n/a
Chestnut-flanked White (Fawn Form)	Cock	white	dark	185c	4645c	149c	white	white with 4645c lines
	Hen	white	dark	1655c	4645c	n/a	white	n/a
Chestnut-flanked White (Grey Form)	Cock	white	dark	185c	425c	149c	white	white with 425c lines
	Hen	white	dark	1655c	425c	n/a	white	n/a
Slate	Cock	white	dark	185c	405c	1525c	404c	404c with 405c lines
	Hen	white	dark	1655c	405c	n/a	404c	n/a
Beige	Cock	white	dark	185c	light brown	1525c	465c	465c with light brown lines
	Hen	white	dark	1655c	light brown	n/a	465c	n/a
Dilute Blue	Cock	white	dark	185c	425c	155c	430c	430c with 425c lines
	Hen	white	dark	1655c	425c	n/a	430c	n/a
Silver	Cock	white	dark	185c	3c	white	1c	1c with 3c lines
	Hen	white	dark	1655c	3c	n/a	1c	n/a
Cream	Cock	white	dark	185c	4675c	white	pale cream	cream with 4675c lines
	Hen	white	dark	1655c	4675c	n/a	pale cream	n/a
Dark Cream	Cock	white	dark	185c	4645c	156c	4665c	4665c with 4645c lines
	Hen	white	dark	1655c	4645c	n/a	4665c	n/a
Cream-backed	Cock	white	dark	185c	4645c	149c	4675c	white with 4645c lines
	Hen	white	dark	1655c	4645c	white	4675c	white
Queensland Isabel	Cock	white	dark	185c	none	1525c	4675c	1c without stripes
	Hen	white	dark	1655c	none	n/a off-white bars	4675c	n/a
White	Cock	white	dark	185c	none	white	white	white
	Hen	white	dark	1655c	none	n/a	white	n/a

Varieties of colour pattern change (Grizzle, Pied, Black-fronted, Black-face, Black-bodied and Yellow-billed) using ground colours of known varieties are not included. Numerals denote Pantone® colour reference.

Breast Bar	Side Flanks	Tail Coverts	Rump	Feet & Legs	Tail	Underparts
black	1675c	black with white bars	white	172c	1 shade lighter than coverts	White to buff towards vent
n/a	n/a	black with white bars	off-white	172c	1 shade lighter than coverts	White to buff towards vent
4625c	1675c	4625c with white bars	white	172c	1 shade lighter than coverts	White to buff towards vent
n/a	n/a	4625c with white bars	off-white	172c	1 shade lighter than coverts	White to buff towards vent
black	1675c	black with white bars	white	172c	2 shades lighter than coverts	White
n/a	n/a	black with white bars	white	172c	2 shades lighter than coverts	White
4645c	472c	4645c with white bars	white	172c	2 shades lighter than coverts	White
n/a	n/a	4645c with white bars	white	172c	2 shades lighter than coverts	White
425c	472c	425c with white bars	white	172c	2 shades lighter than coverts	White
n/a	n/a	n/a	white	172c	(same as cock)	White
405c	1675c	405c with white bars	white	172c	1 shade lighter than coverts	White to buff towards vent
n/a	n/a	405c with white bars	off-white	172c	1 shade lighter than coverts	White to buff towards vent
light brown	1675c	light brown with white bars	white	172c	2 shades lighter than coverts	White to buff towards vent
n/a	n/a	light brown with white bars	off-white	172c	2 shades lighter than coverts	White to buff towards vent
425c	472c	425c with white bars	white	172c	2 shades lighter than coverts	White to buff towards vent
n/a	n/a	425c with white bars	off-white	172c	2 shades lighter than coverts	White to buff towards vent
3c	475c	3c with white bars	white	172c	2 shades lighter than coverts	White to buff towards vent
n/a	n/a	3c with white bars	off-white	172c	2 shades lighter than coverts	White to buff towards vent
4675c	475c	4675c with white bars	white	172c	2 shades lighter than coverts	White to buff towards vent
n/a	n/a	4675c with white bars	off-white	172c	2 shades lighter than coverts	White to buff towards vent
4645c	4715c	4645c with white bars	white	172c	2 shades lighter than coverts	White to buff towards vent
n/a	n/a	4645c with white bars	off-white	172c	2 shades lighter than coverts	White to buff towards vent
4645c	472c	4645c with white bars	white	172c	2 shades lighter than coverts	White
white	4675c	4645c with white bars	off-white	172c	2 shades lighter than coverts	White
no bar	1675c	482c with off-white bars	light cream	172c	Light cream	Buff
n/a	n/a	482c with	off-white	172c	Light cream	Buff
white	white	white	white	172c	White	White
n/a	n/a	white	white	172c	White	White

Page 91

REFERENCES

Birkhead, T.R., 1987. *Sperm Storage Glands in a Passerine: The Zebra Finch Poephila guttata (Estrildidae)*, Journal of the Zoological Society of London Vol. 212, pp.103–108.

Birkhead, T.R., Hunter, F.M., Pellat, J.E., 1989. *Sperm Competition in the Zebra Finch Taeniopygia guttata*, Animal Behaviour Vol. 38, pp. 935–950.

Birkhead, T.R., Møller, A.P., 1992. *Sperm Competition in Birds*, Academic Press, London.

Birkhead, T.R., Pellat, J.E., Fletcher, F., 1993. *Selection and Utilisation of Spermatozoa in the Reproductive Tract of the Hen Zebra Finch Taeniopygia guttata*, Journal of Reproduction and Fertility Vol. 99, pp. 593–600.

Burley, N., 1986a. *Comparison of Band Colour Preferences of Two Species of Estrildid Finches*, Animal Behaviour Vol. 34, pp. 1732–1741.

Burley, N., 1986b. *Sex-ratio Manipulation in Colour Banded Populations of Zebra Finches*, Evolution Vol. 40, pp. 1191–1206.

Burley, N.T., Enstrom, D.A., Chitwood, L., 1994. *Extra-pair Relations in Zebra Finches: Differential Cock Success Results from Hen Tactics*, Animal Behaviour Vol 48, pp. 1031–1041.

Burley, N., Krantzberg, G., Radman, P., 1982. *Influence of Colour Banding on the Conspecific Preferences of Zebra Finches*, Animal Behaviour Vol 10, pp. 444–455.

Cade, T.J., Tobin, C.A., Gold, A., 1965. *Water Economy and Metabolism of Two Estrildid Finches*, Physiological Zoology Vol. 38, pp. 9–33.

Carr, R.A., Zann, R.A., 1986. *The Morphological Identification of Domesticated Zebra Finches, Poephila guttata (Passeriformes: Estrildidae), in Australia*, Australian Journal of Zoology Vol 34, pp. 439–448.

Christidis, L., 1987a. *Biochemical Systematics within Paleotropic Finches (Aves: Estrildidae)*, Auk Vol. 104, pp. 380–392.

Christidis, L., 1987b. *Phylogeny and Systematics of Estrildine Finches and their Relationships to Other Seed-eating Passerines*, Emu Vol. 87, pp. 119–123.

Doneley, B., 1996. *Control and Therapy of Diseases of Birds*, Series A, No. 21, The T G Hungerford Vade Mecum Series for Domestic Animals, University of Sydney.

Goodwin, D., 1982. *Estrildid Finches of the World*, London: British Museum (Natural History), Oxford University Press, Oxford.

Haywood, S., Perrins, C.M., 1992. *Is Clutch Size in Birds Affected by Environmental Conditions During Growth?* Proceedings of the Royal Society (London), Series B 249, pp. 195–197.

Keast, A., 1981. *The Evolutionary Biogeography of Australian Birds*, In Keast, A. (ed.), Ecological Biogeography of Australia Vol. 3, pp. 1586–1635, Dr W. Junk, The Hague.

Lemon, W.C., 1993. *The Energetics of Lifetime Reproductive Success in the Zebra Finch Taeniopygia guttata*, Physiological Zoology Vol. 66, 946–963.

Macwhirter, P., 1994. *Everybird: A Guide to Bird Health*, Inkarta Press, Melbourne.

Müller, A.P., 1990. *Fluctuating Asymmetry in Cock Ornaments may Reliably Reveal Cock Quality*, Animal Behaviour Vol. 40, pp. 1185–1187.

Olsen, G.H., and Orosz, S.E., 2000. *Manual of Avian Medicine*, Mosby Inc., St. Louis, USA.

Roper, A., 1993. *The Structure of the Zebra Finch (i) Begging Call as a Function of Sex, Age and Motivation*, Honours Thesis, La Trobe University.

Schodde, R., 1982. *Origin, Adaptation and Evolution of Birds in Arid Australia*, In Barker, W.R., Greenslade, P.J.M., (eds), Evolution of the Flora and Fauna of Arid Australia, Peacock Publications, Adelaide, pp. 191–224.

Sossinka, R., 1970. *Domestikationserscheinungen beim Zebrafinken Taeniopygia guttata castanotis (Gould)*, Jahrbücher Abteilung f.r Systematik Okologie und Geographie der Tiere Vol. 97, pp. 455–521.

Swaddle, J.P., Cuthill, I.C., 1994. *Preference for Symmetric Cocks by Hen Zebra Finches*, Nature (London) Vol. 367, pp. 165–166.

Zann, R., 1994. *Reproduction in a Zebra Finch Colony in Southeastern Australia: The Significance of Monogamy, Precocial Breeding and Multiple Broods in a Highly Mobile Species*, Emu Vol. 94, pp. 285–299.

Zann, R., 1996. *The Zebra Finch, A Synthesis of Field and Laboratory Studies*, Oxford University Press, Oxford.

Zann, R., Straw, B., 1984. *Feeding Ecology and Breeding of Zebra Finches in Farmland in Northern Victoria*, Australian Wildlife Research Vol. 11, pp. 533–552.

Simply the best publications on pet & aviary birds available ...

BirdKeeper MAGAZINE

Six glossy, colourful and informative issues per year. Featuring articles written by top breeders and avian veterinarians from all over the world.

SUBSCRIPTIONS AVAILABLE

For subscription rates and FREE catalogue contact **ABK Publications** - details on page 96

Handbook of Birds, Cages & Aviaries

This handbook provides a complete overview to the selection, keeping, management and care of both pet and aviary birds from individual pets to larger aviary complexes. Topics include Choosing your Bird, Choosing and Keeping Pet Birds, Housing and Keeping Aviary Birds, Aviary Design, Construction and Management, Plantscaping your Aviary, Nutrition and Feeding, Breeding and Husbandry, General Management and Health and Disease Aspects. A must for the novice and serious aviculturist and all pet bird owners.

ISBN NUMBER 0 9587102 95   Edited by: ABK Publications

The Acclaimed 'A Guide to...' series.

■ **A Guide to Australian White Cockatoos**

Richly illustrated and full of practical hints, this well-researched, well-written book features facets of the author's personal experience which shine throughout its pages. It is sure to become a standard handbook for the breeders and keepers of these unique and magnificent birds, both in Australia and overseas. Species featured are the Sulphur-crested Cockatoo, Short-billed Corella, Eastern Long-billed Corella, Major Mitchell's Cockatoo and Galah.

Contents: Management, Housing, Feeding and Nutrition, Breeding, Diseases and Disorders Common to Cockatoos, Species Profile covering Distribution, Subspecies, Sexing, Breeding, General Comments and Mutations.

ISBN NUMBER   0 9577024 1 8   Author: Chris Hunt.

The Acclaimed 'A Guide to...' series.

■ **A Guide to Australian Grassfinches**
The popularity of Australian Grassfinches worldwide is largely due to the hardiness of these tiny, gregarious and colourful birds. Some 18 species of Grassfinch that are all members of the family Estrildae are recognised in Australia. General topics covered include - Acquiring Birds, Quarantine, Nutrition, Housing, Compatibility and Regulating the Breeding Season, to name just a few. A must for every Finch breeders' library.
ISBN NUMBER 0 9587102 28 Author: Russell Kingston

■ **A Guide to Neophema and Psephotus Grass Parrots and Their Mutations (Revised Edition)**
Bourke's Parrot, Turquoisine Parrot, Scarlet-chested Parrot, Elegant Parrot, Blue-winged Parrot, Rock Parrot, Orange-bellied Parrot, Red-rumped Parrot, Mulga Parrot, Blue-bonnet, Hooded Parrot, Golden-shouldered Parrot and Paradise Parrot.
ISBN NUMBER 0 9587102 44 Author: Toby Martin

■ **A Guide to Asiatic Parrots and Their Mutations (Revised Edition)**
Alexandrine Parrot, Plum-headed Parrot, Indian Ringnecked Parrot, Derbyan Parrot, Malabar Parrot, Slaty-headed Parrot, Malayan Long-tailed Parrot, Blossom-headed Parrot and Moustache Parrot.
ISBN NUMBER 0 9587102 52 Authors: Syd & Jack Smith

■ **A Guide to Australian Long and Broad-tailed Parrots and New Zealand Kakarikis**
Crimson-winged Parrot, Princess Parrot, Regent Parrot, Superb Parrot, King Parrot, Red-capped Parrot, Mallee Ringnecked Parrot, Cloncurry Parrot, Port Lincoln Parrot, Twenty-eight Parrot, Red-fronted Parrot and Yellow-fronted Parrot.
ISBN NUMBER 0 9587455 36 Author: Kevin Wilson

■ **A Guide to Rosellas and Their Mutations**
Eastern Rosella, Tasmania Eastern Rosella, Golden-mantled Rosella, Pale-headed Rosella, Blue-cheeked Rosella, Northern Rosella, Kimberley Northern Rosella, Western Rosella, Red-backed Western Rosella, Crimson Rosella, Northern Crimson Rosella, Yellow Rosella, Adelaide Rosella, Tasmanian Rosella.
ISBN NUMBER 0 9587455 52 Author: Australian Birdkeeper

■ **A Guide to Eclectus Parrots**
A comprehensive look at the keeping, breeding, housing, health and management of these beautiful parrots, including hand-rearing tips.
ISBN NUMBER 0 9587455 44 Author: Australian Birdkeeper

■ **A Guide to Gouldian Finches and Their Mutations**
Covers all requirements to successfully breed and maintain Gouldians including concise information on health, nutrition and colour mutations.
ISBN NUMBER 0 9587455 60 Authors: John Sammut & Dr Rob Marshall

- **A Guide to Cockatiels and Their Mutations**
  Written by two of Australia's foremost Cockatiel breeders, the book features beautiful colour photography, including all known mutations. Excellent easy-to-read information covers the care, management, housing and breeding of these popular birds.
  ISBN NUMBER 0 9587455 87 Authors: Peggy Cross and Diana Andersen

- **A Guide to Pigeons, Doves and Quail**
  A world first in aviculture, this book covers all species in this group available to the Australian aviculturist. Stunning colour photography throughout is supported by precise, easy-to-read information on the care, management, health and breeding of these unique birds.
  ISBN NUMBER 0 6462305 81 Author: Danny Brown

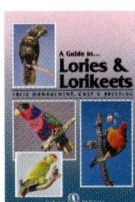
- **A Guide to Lories and Lorikeets**
  Recognised internationally as a specialist lory/lorikeet breeder, Peter Odekerken is also well-known for his superb photography. This title exemplifies Peter's great love and understanding of these unique and colourful, brush-tongued psittacines.
  ISBN NUMBER 0 9587445 95 Author: Peter Odekerken

- **A Guide to Basic Health and Disease in Birds**
  From finches to macaws, Mike discusses common diseases to be aware of, quarantine procedures, recognising health problems, to basic steps required to maintain healthy birds. A must for novice and experienced aviculturists alike.
  ISBN NUMBER 0 6462305 73 Author: Dr Mike Cannon

- **A Guide to Incubation & Handraising Parrots**
  This title covers all the necessary requirements needed to successfully take an egg through to a fully weaned chick. Beautifully illustrated with colour images throughout, this valuable title also includes many charts and diagrams and informative text laid out in the easy-to-read format. An invaluable reference for any serious bird breeder.
  ISBN NUMBER 0 9587102 1 X Author: Phil Digney

- **A Guide to Pet & Companion Birds**
  This informative and colourful 96 page book guides you through selecting a bird, housing, feeding and caring for that bird, understanding its behaviour, health aspects, taming, training, behavioural problems and how to approach increasing your flock. A must for *every* bird owner.
  ISBN NUMBER 0 9587266 12 Authors: Ray Dorge and Gail Sibley

- **A Guide to Pheasants & Waterfowl**
  Author of the highly regarded A Guide to Pigeons, Doves & Quail, Dr Danny Brown has produced this superlative new title on pheasants and waterfowl. The informative easy-to-read text is lavishly supported with beautiful colour images throughout. Covering all aspects of caring, housing, management and breeding of these unique birds, this new title is a credit to the author and an ideal reference source.
  ISBN NUMBER 0 9587102 36 Author: Dr Danny Brown

Publishers' Note

This title is published by **ABK Publications** who produce a wide and varied range of avicultural literature including the world acclaimed **Australian Birdkeeper** magazine - a full colour, bi-monthly magazine specifically designed for birdlovers and aviculturists. It is the intention of the publishers to produce high quality, informative literature for birdlovers, fanciers and aviculturists alike throughout the world. It is also the publishers' belief that the dissemination of qualified information on the care, keeping and breeding of birds is imperative for the total well-being of captive birds and the increased knowledge of aviculturists.

Nigel Steele-Boyce

Nigel Steele-Boyce
Publisher/Editor-In-Chief
ABK Publications

For further information or Free Catalogue contact:

ABK Publications
P.O. Box 6288
South Tweed Heads
NSW 2486 Australia

Phone: (07) 5590 7777 Fax: (07) 5590 7130
Email: birdkeeper@birdkeeper.com.au
http://www.birdkeeper.com.au